ON
BEING
MEMORABLE

Nine Keys for Exceptional Change

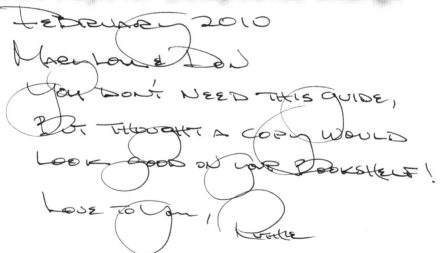

RUTHIE H. DEARING

ISBN: 1-4392-7037-6
EAN13: 9781439270370

PRAISE FOR ON BEING MEMORABLE

This book is recommended to anyone running for public office. On Being Memorable contains an excellent set of exercises to put you on the right track to public service for all the best and most rewarding reasons. It's a win-win...you become memorable because of your contribution to your community and your community benefits from your service!

Pat Giardina Carpenter
President
The WISH List (Women In the Senate and House)

For each person, the pursuit of purposeful, worthwhile work is a goal as we mature in our careers. The bridge from pursuit of success to significance is crossed in youth but for most later in life as we reflect on the culture, needs and tensions so obvious and prevalent. For some, the bridge is never crossed. This book provides a map to navigate the bridge-crossing for those willing to take the journey from success to significance.

Paul H. Keckley, Ph.D.
Executive Director
Deloitte Center for Health Solutions
Washington DC

Where was this book when I was younger? Ruthie Dearing has encapsulated wisdom from many years of experience into a series of principles that if applied will change your life, your relationships, and your future. Don't just read this book – study and apply it. You'll never regret your decision to do so.

Walt Larimore, M.D.
Co-author of **His Brain, Her Brain:**
How divinely designed differences can strengthen your marriage

ON BEING MEMORABLE
Nine Keys for Exceptional Change

SPIRITUAL TRANSFORMATION

Today, for many of us, self-discovery and development is a way of life. As we struggle for answers to challenging and difficult issues or problems in our lives, we read lots of self-development books and learn from self-help gurus on television so that we will know exactly what to do.

Many books and programs are designed to appeal to the American concept of "before and after"—the rags to riches story. Where, with just the right suggestion or strategy, we believe we can make dramatic changes and turn everything around in just a matter of days or weeks. Unfortunately, in reality, lasting change does not usually occur after reading a book and practicing a couple of times, or watching a motivational speaker talking about methods of change. According to a study by John Norcross, PhD, a professor of psychology in Pennsylvania, of the 40 to 45 percent of the people who make resolutions on New Years Day, only one-half will succeed in six months.

However, when we make a serious commitment to transform our lives, it is possible to do so. Norcross says that among individuals who actively attempt to make a significant change, 70–80 percent of the people are ultimately successful. Interestingly, he notes that it may take two to ten tries for these individuals to accomplish their goals.

The big issue for many of us is the understanding that change does not just happen—change is a process. To make changes, to improve our behavior takes time—time to decide what to do and time to make the change. Change of any kind is not an event. Change is not something that we do, and once it is done, it is complete.

Change is a process that goes on and on, up and down, and over and over. So it is never ending.

What transformation do you want to make? How willing are you to be awakened to who you are or who you wish to be? What are you called to be or do?

Often, when we make a significant transformation or change in our life, it is due to a great challenge or time of difficulty that we experience. All of us have a history comprised of the experiences that have occurred. These experiences come into play when we initiate change or make a transformation—an alteration in the way we live our lives. For many, in fact, for almost all of us, a great or terrible tragedy has occurred at some point in our lives. As we move on, the way that we face this difficulty and how we overcome the challenge gives us the courage, the resilience, and the lessons we need to make our life transformation.

I think this transformation is a spiritual journey—a journey that often leads us to believe in some outside being, a higher power—some entity that influences and helps us change. As noted above, most of us are forced into change by difficult or challenging circumstances that cause us pain. But this pain tells us that everything is not right and that changes are needed. The pain and the decision to make change often initiates or influences our pathways to spiritual awakening. We have to first acknowledge that we want to behave or live in a different way or with different responses and reactions. And second, we have to identify and find the resources we need to make the changes needed to transform our lives. We must be willing to embrace risk and change, even when it is difficult or when we fear the outcome. There is always a silver lining; good exists even in challenging and painful experiences.

So whatever challenge or difficulty you are going through, know that you have the ability to manage or transform your life. You have the courage, energy, strength, flexibility, and perseverance to do what is needed to make the changes that you seek and desire. You are capable of surmounting the most difficult steps and obstacles as you transform your life and achieve even greater goals.

Alice says, "Would you tell me please, which way
I ought to go from here?"

"That depends a good deal on where you want to
get to," said the Cat.

"I don't care much where ..."

"Then, it doesn't matter which way you go," said the Cat.

"*—so long as I get somewhere,*" Alice added.

Alice's Adventures in Wonderland
Lewis Carroll

Alice walks through a tiny door that is seemingly impossible to enter …

a door so small it can easily be overlooked.

Here are nine keys to help guide you toward

opening the door that will lead
to a distinguished life

filled with interesting experiences
and adventures.

CHAPTER ONE

UNLOCKING YOUR POTENTIAL
FOR BEING MEMORABLE

What Causes Someone to Be Memorable or Unforgettable?
Stop and think for a minute about the people whom you
have met or had contact with over the past two weeks.
Has someone impressed you, either positively or negatively?
It may be a new acquaintance, a co-worker on a project,
or a salesperson. Something about this person causes her
or him to be remembered. Whatever occurred, this person
stands out in your mind and is remembered. For whatever
reason, apart from everyone else you have interacted with
or observed during the past few weeks, this person comes
to mind when you recall people with whom you have had
contact. That's a pretty powerful impression.

Something about the person made him or her
unforgettable and memorable. What was it that
impressed you? Chances are that the first images you
recall are what you saw or heard, combined with a feeling
or emotion about the experience. Take a few moments
to recall the person and the situation, remembering the
first things that come to mind. Some of the things you may
remember could include the following:

- A sincere compliment or greeting, given
  spontaneously and with pleasure

- Positive self-confidence and ease with others

- A glowing smile for everyone from a mail clerk to the
  president

- A voice that conveys sincerity and warmth

- A warm, personal note written specifically for you

- Someone who uses his or her spare time in an
  unusual or constructive way

- Someone who treats another person very well or very badly
- Someone who overreacted at an important meeting
- A presentation that progressed like a piece of classical music
- Someone who stood up for an important, but controversial issue
- A well-written office memo, or conversely, a letter with poor grammar and several typos
- An appealing and inviting laugh that makes you smile and want to laugh along
- A polished personal presentation or the opposite

We can all recall someone who created a memorable impression in our minds. If you think about this impression and the person, you will realize that the memory you hold is not an accident. Personal presence and credibility do not just happen. But neither are they like a suit of clothing, available for one occasion, but not another. Personal presence and credibility must be carefully developed, without flaws, gaps, or inconsistencies. Once in place, personal presence and credibility are with us throughout our lives, in all situations and experiences.

To establish a memorable personal presence, creditable behavior requires an ongoing focus and concentration. Being memorable must be worked on until it becomes a permanent part of your persona and your life, regardless of what you are wearing or doing. Being memorable necessitates a refocusing of your thinking and your behaviors to assure that a positive memory follows you. However, the residual effect of leaving a positive, unforgettable memory is not always possible. No one is perfect, and thus positive outcomes aren't always achievable. Yet for each of us, our overall goal is to always be perceived positively and remembered well.

One memory that comes to mind helps to keep me focused. Several years ago, I was in a shop, trying to conclude a purchase quickly. In doing so, I reacted somewhat rudely to the clerk who when seeing my name on the check said, "Oh, aren't you the woman who gives those talks on how to be positive and memorable?" Suddenly, I was slowed to a crawl and quietly responded that yes, I was that person. The clerk looked me over and stated that "Maybe you need to learn how to do what you say." I told her that I agreed and thanked her for her input. Wow! What a quick lesson about learning that regardless of where you are or what you are doing, being memorable must be worked on until it becomes a permanent part of your life.

Being memorable requires a commitment to always being thoughtful or intentional—every minute—until it becomes a part of your natural thinking, your reactions and behaviors, your inner self. If this sounds unachievable, think again! *On Being Memorable* offers a new approach, the STAR Approach **(Success Through Attribute Reinforcement)**, a method that can help you achieve this goal. From past experiences, I can boldly say that the STAR Approach is motivating, self-renewing, and self-rewarding.

On reflection, it becomes readily apparent that in order to establish a positive, memorable image, we must change direction and refocus our energies. We must heighten our awareness of what it means to be an extraordinary person. We must develop ways of thinking and behaving that reinforces this perception in our minds and in the minds of others.

Impressions Last
Unlike Alice, the majority of us are not content to simply "get somewhere." We want to do great things, contribute to the good of society, and be wonderfully successful while making a memorable impression.

Secretly, each of us wants to make a positive impression—a wonderful, memorable, and unforgettable impression—perhaps even a distinct impression, to be perceived as an "extraordinary" individual. We want others (especially valued others) to remember what we did, what we said, and who we are in ways that last over time. From early childhood, when we are told to "act nice and mind your manners," and continuing into our adult lives where our goals are to become Prince Charming, replicate Cinderella, or land a great job, much of our energy is focused in pursuit of our wish to create this memorable impression. For some, being unforgettable is being gracious and charming, or witty and urbane in our comments, to creatively decorate ourselves or our home, to give to others without concern for our own needs.

Although the dictionary definitions of the words *memorable* and *extraordinary* are not the same, their meaning, as related to being memorable or extraordinary, is similar. *Memorable* is described as "likely or worthy to be remembered." The word *unforgettable* is described as being "incapable of being forgotten" or memorable. *Extraordinary* is to be "exceptional to a marked extent; to be striking, imposing, notable, or surprising; to be out of the usual course." Thus, if one is exceptional to a marked extent, striking, notable, or surprising, one is extraordinary, and most certainly memorable and unforgettable!

Much has been written and said about how to dress correctly, how to speak well and listen aggressively, and the importance of feeling good about ourselves. Although many of us have read several books promoting the advantages of these skills and diligently practiced many of the recommended strategies, we may still feel that something is lacking. Something seems to be missing.

After considerable reflection, it seems a different approach is needed—one that focuses specifically on the end goal we all dream about—to be remembered as someone unique, distinctive, and extraordinary. To accomplish this goal, to become a memorable, unforgettable person, I have developed an approach that focuses on magnification of the positive attributes, behaviors, and skills we each have developed.

This approach is called the **STAR Approach—Success Through Attribute Reinforcement**. Rather than expending energy to eliminate negative behaviors or habits, focus instead on building and strengthening your best talents and skills. Using the STAR Approach, you can highlight positive behavioral attributes in the same way that you highlight or draw attention to your best physical characteristics. We all have positive attributes, but we don't always know how to make the most of them. The STAR Approach helps you define your desired attributes and develop a plan to create the memorable persona you wish to develop. To distinguish the STAR Approach from other change strategies that have been repeatedly tried, an in-depth, soul-searching introspection and honest appraisal are required. You need to ask yourself two key questions: What are your motives? What do you hope to gain?

A Reason for Change

Let's face it; regardless of whether we know or admit it, the majority of us are unwilling to work on changing for the sole purpose of being a better person. Introspection and honesty will tell us that we don't work at changing our thoughts and behaviors or improving our attributes, presentation, and abilities just to be better or brighter. When we honestly acknowledge the reasons why we try to change, to be different (better), what is revealed, beneath all of our thoughts and feelings, is our desire to be memorable and unforgettable. In our minds and hearts, we believe that making changes will bring accomplishment of many things: improved lifestyle, increased happiness, rewards, notice, and recognition.

When we look honestly at our motivation to change, we discover two fundamental reasons that force action. We change to gain or achieve a desired objective, or we change to avoid or prevent a loss.

Some examples of how and why we change to achieve a desired objective or prevent a loss are:

- We sign up to finish our college degree or take additional education classes that make us more marketable and better skilled.

- We resolve to eat less fatty foods and more veggies and fruit so that we can drop ten pounds.

- We agree to take on an extra project at work and give our manager solid support.

- We happily agree to accompany our partner to an event he or she wants to see, but has no interest for us.

- We give up cigarettes, excessive drinking, or overspending.

To use the STAR Approach **(Success Through Attribute Reinforcement)**, we need to understand how we have tried to create a positive impression in the past. Standard operating procedure for most of us has been to work on or fix one or two specific behaviors, traits, or skills. We believe that improvement of these separate parts will make a significant difference in our lives and in the way others perceive us. This traditional thinking carries the assumption that incremental or sporadic improvements in our behavior, performance, or appearance will allow us to attain a current goal or capture attention and interest in a positive, distinct way. But goals change as do individuals; therefore, change to achieve a simple goal becomes obsolete.

In the past, we also believed that by improving separate aspects of our behavior or appearance, a bit here, a lot there, a noticeable difference in the overall image would occur and distinguish each of us in a memorable way. This expectation, that by changing certain aspects or characteristics and hoping a dramatic shift in our total image will magically occur, is wishful thinking. Certainly the change we make may be noticeable or distinguishing, but too often, the change is overshadowed by inconsistencies in the overall picture. This incongruity can offset the full benefit the change may provide, or even worse, create a discordant effect that hurts our image.

What we haven't taken into account is that there is seldom a one-to-one change between new or different behavior and the perceptions that others hold of us. A person's perception of us doesn't change just because we change one or more behaviors or improve some of our interactive skills. We may have forgotten this lesson, but we learned this when we were kids. The playground bully wasn't accepted as a friend just because he stopped slapping us around for a few days. It actually took considerable time and long-term consistent behavioral change before we even began to consider that the bully was a different person. We perceived that the old behavior was still lurking beneath the surface, and we looked for reasons to explain the bully's new behavior, while our perceptions of him remained unchanged.

Initial Assessment

If you are not fully conscious of the ways in which you project yourself in all situations, you are not giving yourself the opportunity to create an unforgettable and memorable presence. Assessment and evaluation of your present image will define areas for change that result in small improvements and dramatic differences in your career, in business and social activities, and in your personal life.

The following examples clarify this point:

- *Persistence/determination/diligence*: A willingness to complete projects that will enhance or expand your life

- *Caring/concern/fervent*: Listening with eagerness and interest to others

- *Enthusiasm/zeal/directed*: Displaying a passion for achieving or fulfilling your life mission

- *Empowered/attain/confident*: Believing that you can accomplish anything you choose to do

- *Stable/unwavering/committed*: Remaining grounded and focused in spite of negative circumstances or devastating odds

To increase your awareness and establish guidelines to help define your goals, complete this simple exercise. Take a few minutes and think about your present image. How do others perceive and see you? If someone who works with you or knows you well is asked to describe you by identifying your attributes or behavioral characteristics, what will he or she say? List below the five attributes that you believe are representative of you and the image you now project as perceived by others.

_____

_____

_____

_____

_____

Now, put this list aside. We will use it later in the following chapter to identify the characteristics and attributes that you seek in order to create a more memorable and unforgettable image.

The STAR Approach
Using the STAR Approach **(Success Through Attribute Reinforcement)** for personal change and image building, a realignment of the emphasis given to your energy and effort is suggested. Instead of trying to randomly fix different parts, you must clearly identify and define the overall picture of the extraordinary individual you wish to be, and then concentrate your efforts on making that picture a reality.

To further clarify the difference provided by this approach, the following table illustrates the motivations and outcomes commonly adopted to change our behavior or attitude. Think about it. Where are you on this table? Where will you be in the future when you make a commitment to becoming the memorable person you want to be and can be?

MOTIVATIONS AND OUTCOMES

PERCENT PARTICIPATING	FOCUS OF IMPROVEMENT	MOTIVATION	GOALS
1st Level			
As far as 75% of the people ever get	Goals are vague with undefined wants – just "want to be/do better, to get along, to be okay"	External: want what others have, but no specific or long-term goal to achieve; Internal: a "hope" that change will bring positive results	To randomly or haphazardly improve specific behaviors or bodily appearance

PERCENT PARTICIPATING	FOCUS OF IMPROVEMENT	MOTIVATION	GOALS
2nd Level			
Top 25% will achieve with the help of seminars, workshops or counseling	Goals are clearly and specifically defined, but limiting because compartmentalized	External: to get along better with others; to prevent failure or negative responses from others; Internal: to be more effective; to get a promotion or raise; to develop happier relationships with family and friends	To change a number of behaviors, one by one, but without a comprehensive picture or plan of the overall result
3rd Level			
Top 10% may get this far with a mentor	Goals are specifically defined and conceptualized through a plan of action	External: to achieve a higher level of personal/ professional success Internal: to achieve self fulfillment and a personal sense of accomplishment	To change thoughts, feelings & behaviors to prevent occasionally occurring minor and, rarely occurring, major glitches in image
4th Level			
Top 3-5% achieves this level. With the STAR Approach, almost anyone can achieve this level	Goals are clear, vivid and compelling, visual picture is identified and defined; comprehensive plan for change is developed and adopted in all areas of life	External: to stand out and make a difference; Internal: acknowledge desire for recognition, reward and self fulfillment based on personal growth and contribution	To dramatically change the perception of others; to match external image with internal picture of self as extra-ordinary/ memorable individual; to be a star

5th Level

Top 1% achieve this level	Goals precisely defined and permanently etched in consciousness	External: contribute to the good of others; serve as a guide or mentor; Internal: sees role as a mission in life	To achieve higher emotional and spiritual growth; to make a significant and memorable contribution to the lives of others

After reviewing the Motivations and Outcomes Table, where do you place yourself today? Are you at the level you wish to be? Are you getting all of the results and rewards that you seek in life? If you are, call me. I'd love to know your secret. But if you're like most of us and you're still seeking fulfillment, read on!

The key to mastering the fourth level requires you to develop a mental blueprint of what you expect, desire, and demand of yourself before you begin to make changes. To develop your mental blueprint, you will need to work through the process outlined on the following pages. Your blueprint must form a clear, vivid, compelling picture of your goal. Each day you must mentally visit the picture to confirm and reaffirm your goal. The image you desire for yourself has to be crystal clear in your mind so that it is available for use throughout the day. For some of us, this image may even occur in our dreams at night.

Each of us has different levels of motivation or different incentives for accomplishing a goal. In a sermon on the *Hour of Power*, Reverend Robert Schuler talked about the importance of goals in our lives. Because our goals empower us, goals are drivers or motivators of action. Schuler says that in order to create an empowering energy, the goal must have four characteristics:

- The goal must be meaningful (to you and in your life).

- The goal must be marvelous (people will marvel at your accomplishment).

- The goal must be measurable (there are specific objectives and time frames).

- The goal must be manageable (you can accomplish it without detriment).

Often, we see something that we want, but if we do not believe the object or goal is attainable, we will not do what is needed to get it. You must draw upon your inner confidence so that you will know this goal is attainable—you *can* become a memorable person! In order to succeed, you must have a compelling desire (not a hope or a wish) for a new image and a crystal-clear vision of the image you desire. You must believe your goal is possible, and not just a hyped-up daydream. Where are you going? What are you called to be?

How do you build this driving mental image of your future self? You begin by making a solid desire and commitment to change and by implementing the STAR Approach **(Success Through Attribute Reinforcement)** into your life. When applied with discipline and commitment, the STAR Approach works through reinforcement of attributes and will help you attain your goal effectively and completely.

The stronger your level of expectation, the greater will be your success. To establish a compelling desire, you must build your inner confidence. Believe in yourself and keep telling yourself that you can achieve your goal or the objective you seek. Willpower and persistent follow-through are essential requirements. You must believe in yourself. You must think about and reinforce the positive qualities and strengths you possess.

Inner confidence will help you open your mind to see things differently and to see with a clearer or more expansive view. Self-belief means that you accept yourself and open your mind and thoughts to being happy and grateful for what you have. Everyone else is not smarter, prettier, stronger, or more talented.

Think positively about yourself and reinforce your strengths and skills, and begin to take small risks—apply for the higher position; wave to your new neighbor; smile at the person coming out as you enter the building; give a compliment to the co-worker you dislike. Confront your fears and believe in yourself!

In the STAR Approach **(Success Through Attribute Reinforcement)**, there are three steps that are needed to identify your desired image. The overall process for implementing the STAR Approach is fully described in Chapter Two. Look at the Process Diagram as you read through steps 1, 2, and 3 noted in the "Summary Thoughts" at the end of this chapter. Use the process diagram to help by writing reference points for each step.

PROCESS DIAGRAM

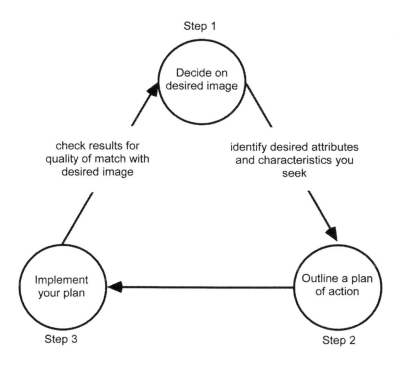

13

A New Approach to Change

Using the STAR Approach **(Success Through Attribute Reinforcement)** for change and personal growth is different. Rather than focusing on fixing or eliminating a weakness or fault, concentrated efforts to highlight and build your strengths will dramatically increase your success. Using the STAR Approach, you can cut in half the time and effort needed to create the image you desire.

Why is this? Throughout our lives, we learned the traditional approach, "first, fix the negatives." And yet, this approach is not the most efficient or effective way to change. Our energies and efforts are depleted by trying NOT to do certain things, rather than initiating a new approach. When we attempt to fix our weaknesses first, we create a host of difficult learning tasks. In addition, the time before we experience satisfaction and accomplishment is lengthened. In fact, focusing your efforts on fixing negative attributes or behaviors is counter motivational until significant changes are made. Conversely, using the STAR Approach of working on the positive aspects or attributes in your life will quickly bring the results you seek.

Everyone can make an immediate change in his or her lifestyle. A friend tells a story about her seven year-old grandson who was enjoying a family brunch. When asked what he wanted to drink, he expressed a desire for a soda. After consuming half of the can, he read the nutrition facts on the label and then offered the drink to others at the table. When asked why he didn't want to finish it, he stated that he was concerned about the amount of carbohydrate in the drink and was being more careful about the amount of sugar he was eating. No one drank the rest of the soda!

The training of Olympic athletes has demonstrated some of the advantages gained by using existing strengths to alter or enhance behaviors. One of the most powerful psycho-emotional reasons involves the dynamics of concentric growth. Concentric growth demonstrates the theory of physics that the addition of "new" matter or something new will displace or remove existing matter or negative behaviors and characteristics. Through the concentric growth dynamic, as you increase or enhance existing strengths, they multiply and expand their connections, producing new strengths or skills. By using your existing strengths more, you will actually displace your weaknesses, like putting rocks into water. As the rocks are added, the water is displaced. Through concentric growth, the increased use and expansion of your strengths overshadows and actually displaces the negatives or weaknesses in your behavior, without diminishing your energy while you work to eliminate the negatives.

This approach does not mean that all negative behaviors or traits are eliminated or managed solely through displacement. Your evaluation and self-assessment will identify some negative behaviors that you must concentrate on ending or stopping. To change your image, you must give up old habits and behaviors that conflict with the desired image you seek. However, at this point, the main focus of your efforts should be to increase, build, and highlight positive attributes, characteristics and traits.

Equally as important, begin now to subtly, overtly, and completely change your thoughts and feelings when they do not coincide with your desired image or when they damage the desired image you seek to establish. You possess the power of choice; you determine what you think and how you feel. You can choose to be confident and positive, or you can be fearful and worried. Remember, concentrated efforts to highlight and build your strengths will help you make the changes you desire. Over time, as you incorporate the STAR Approach into your life, your desired image will become a reality.

SUMMARY THOUGHTS FROM CHAPTER ONE

Steps to Success
As mentioned before, many of us have focused on making ourselves better by "fixing the negatives." And yet, as many of us know, this approach is not the most efficient or effective way to change. Our energies and efforts are focused on trying **NOT** to do certain things. Begin by focusing your efforts on doing positive good things that bring the results you want. Try it, try it—you will see—you will like it and agree!!!

Step One: Identifying Your Desired Image
You begin by deciding on the image of the extraordinary and memorable individual you want to be. The personal attributes and characteristics that you seek must be identified. You need to create a mental blueprint of the image you desire. Make the blueprint become a compelling image, driven by a clear and vivid picture of the attributes and characteristics you desire in your personality. Using this blueprint, you can define what you will be like, what your behaviors will be, and how you will think and feel as a memorable, extraordinary person.

Step Two: Outline a Plan of Action
To achieve success with any goal, we must determine the process and steps of completion. First, begin by outlining a plan of action that takes the following into account:

a) Your existing positive attributes and personal traits

b) The characteristics, behaviors, or attributes that are missing or need to be enhanced or strengthened

c) Identified behaviors or actions to develop the positive attributes or characteristics you desire

d) Visualized and mapped-out scenarios where you implement the behaviors or actions identified above.

Step Three: Implementation of Your Action Plan

Implement your plan and evaluate your progress. In your daily activities, focus on highlighting your positive attributes and characteristics—your present strengths. Work to make these positive forces bring even greater returns for your efforts while you initiate development of your desired new attributes and behaviors. Focus on the spiritual existence of why you are making the changes you desire; Forget and push aside any selfish reasons you may have for making changes in your life.

Why are you here? What is your calling in life? Take time to reflect on your life—what you are doing and why you are doing it. What can you do to make life better for others and yourself? Remember, the more you give, the more you will get in return.

CHAPTER TWO

UNLOCKING YOUR POTENTIAL FOR AN UNFORGETTABLE OUTCOME

The Process

Most of us have not consciously identified the image we wish to project. We have taken a job, accepted a role, worked hard and often, and without even realizing it, established an image. Now, stop and consider whether you like the image that you project. Do you want to maintain this image? Or do you want to change or modify it? You can create a new image by changing "chance" to "choice."

Regardless of who we are, what we do, or how long we've been trying to do it, we still dream of making a positive unforgettable impression on the people we meet. Through our experiences and the experiences of others, we are convinced that anyone can create a lasting, positive memorable image. Use of the STAR Approach to focus on your strengths and positive behaviors is the foundation upon which a positive image is built.

So if you want to change your image and your secret goal is to be perceived as a memorable person, an extraordinary individual, let's do it! The STAR Approach makes perfect sense.

Step One: Image Identification

You must first decide on the image you wish to have. What image do you wish to promote and convey to others? How do you want people to think of you? The following questions will help identify and define the image you seek. Think about the questions and your answers, and then write out your responses to each question.

1) What is the image you desire? How do you want to be seen and remembered?

2) What behaviors and actions will work to create and reinforce this image?

3) How do you transition from your present image to your desired image?

You may react and say "how cold and calculating" or "how phony." But really think about your present behavior. Don't we all start each day hoping and wanting to be positive, friendly, inspiring, and kind? None of us sets out in the morning to be a grumble-butt, to upset others, or create a negative impression. With established goals and a plan for change, we take the "hit and miss" out of our behavior and actions. Initiating a plan and accomplishing the changes you wish to make will add consistency and bring positive rewards to your life.

Images can be changed, but it will take energy and concentrated work. If you want to change your image, it can be done and quite effectively, too. Anyone can change his or her image. It is a matter of desire, persistence, and positive thinking. When using the STAR Approach to change your image, negative behaviors will be displaced as you expand and increase the positive behaviors of your personality. But you will also have to give up old habits and behaviors that contradict your new image. Ah...the fun part! Now, you must begin to act and react in new and different ways.

For example, think about the image you present when, sitting at a meeting, you hear negative information about the project you are managing. How do you respond?

Do you cross your arms? Do you push your chair back from the table? Do you roll your eyes or frown and stare at the person providing the information? Do you interrupt and begin to angrily defend your actions or behaviors? Your response will certainly influence or affect the reactions of those listening and the person providing the negative information.

I remember a situation where at a meeting I saw one of the doctors react in an annoyed manner and saw that same type of response coming back to him from others at the table. The meeting was interrupted briefly, and during the break, I spoke with the doctor and asked him to slow his thinking process and focus on getting a positive outcome.   He began by apologizing for reacting and asked the person to give more details about her concerns. To remove agitation, the doctor slowly asked questions, took notes, and listened attentively. This response changed the whole tenor of the meeting and provided some very helpful information for the doctor. Acting and reacting in new and different ways can be most valuable to us all.

Personal Style

A large part of your image comes from your personal style. Our personal style is composed of three primary characteristics: our ethical style, our physical style, and our social style. To better understand how personal style is developed and composed, a description of these three primary components follows. These components make up your personal style.

Ethical Style

>	The first is ethical style or the core values in which we believe. Each of us has established our own philosophy and the principles that guide us through

life. However, for many of us, our values and principles have never been clearly defined or crystallized.

For instance, we do not really know how we will respond to certain circumstances if we have never been placed in that situation. For example, how would you decide OJ's innocence or guilt if you were on the jury? If you found $5,000 in the bank parking lot, would you keep the money or take it into the bank? Or if the amount of money found is only $300 and the owner's address is on the envelope, would you return the money? In other circumstances, we may know where we stand on a particular situation or issue, but frequently, even though we hold a defined value or principle, we do not stand behind it. We are afraid of the reactions from others to our opinions or beliefs. We waffle, we have no opinion, or we say what we think others wish to hear. Because of this, our ethical style is mushy or indistinct.

In order to be memorable and unforgettable, you must define your values and identify the principles by which you live your life. And you must be willing to speak out and stand up for these values and principles. At work, you must convince both subordinates and superiors that you possess integrity, dedication, and a sense of fairness. The best way to do this is through the consistent emphasis of these traits in your daily behavior, in the way you react to colleagues and staff members. In your personal life, you must demonstrate this same consistency. Your actions and behaviors must echo your beliefs in the values and principles that define you on a personal level.

Physical Style

The second characteristic is physical style. This style includes the use of movement and your appearance. Physical style may seem obvious, but many people do not fully understand the importance of this element. The way that you walk, use your hands, and look at others reflects your sense of self and of your style. Listening with attention and respect is not only a measure of genuine caring, but of good business and good manners, and it is also an indication of your physical style.

Another part of physical style involves your choice of clothing. The clothing you wear tells a lot about you, often in subtle ways that you may not fully appreciate. Physical style also includes observation of the dress code for a particular organization or situation. This means paying attention to the people with whom you are meeting or to the function you are attending. Dressing appropriately for the occasion is a simple way of showing that you respect the people or organization with whom you are meeting.

Learning how to speak with distinction and authority is also part of your physical style. To be truly effective, you must know the topic about which you are speaking and have all of the information and facts that you need. Be well prepared; be a bit early or on time; be thoughtful and positive in your approach.

Social Style

The third characteristic is social style. Our social style involves more than merely how we relate and interact with friends. Social style also involves our interactions and relationships with other employees, business colleagues, and professional associates. Social style and the way we treat those around us reflect our core values and principles. Our social style tells others not only how much we respect other people, but also how much we respect ourselves. In the chapter on poise, social style is discussed in greater detail.

Having good social style means learning how to interact within the social structure of an organization or a group. Good social style knows when to stay and when to go. It is knowing how to participate in a purely social function and feel comfortable even when you may not have as much experience as others who are present or any interest in the function. Good social style involves the incorporation of grace into your life. Grace, defined in the dictionary as "unrestrained goodwill," is a powerful indicator of the social style you possess.

In order to create personal presence and a positive unforgettable image, you must be conscious of what your style says about you and how your approach affects those around you. Your approach is the way you package and present information to others. Often, when your approach is different from that of your audience, the people listening may not receive the information as positively as you desire. You need to think about the behaviors of your audience and change your approach so that it corresponds favorably. For example, if you are presenting information to a financial person, your information needs to focus on the numbers game. Conversely, if talking with a marketing person, you may wish to stress market research or the way a product may influence or initiate market change. Being observant and tuned into your audience is a key element in creating a positive memorable impression.

Three key elements factor into the approach equation and your method of presentation:

- The things you say to others (the language or tone of voice that conveys your messages)

- The way you speak and listen to others without realizing the impact of the message you send (the nonverbal realm—when you are not directly intending to communicate, but often do through expressions and gestures)

- Your general behavior and actions (is there consistency?), or as the saying goes, "Do you walk what you talk?"

For each of us, the integration and performance of these key elements constitutes our personal style. In essence, our personal style and our approach to life greatly influence our ability to be perceived as memorable, unforgettable, and extraordinary.

Think about how you react when you greet someone you really like who is visiting your home or office. You are smiling, enthusiastic, and giving positive comments to show your enjoyment and appreciation of that person. Conversely, when we welcome someone with whom we do not agree or like, we may not show the same signs exhibited with the good friend as noted above.

A very close and affluent friend who used to live in Dallas is the most capable master of this skill. Carol could host a fabulous event and warmly, graciously welcome guests— those she genuinely liked and some whom she did not like. The outcome of this talented and skillful behavior made

Carol an unforgettable favorite among the social set and assured her a constant stream of invitations. I remember once when Carol was greeting two women for a major social event at her home and was rudely interrupted by another guest. Carol listened, smiling and nodding her head in response, then charmingly complimented this woman with no mention of her interruption. Now, having made her "memorable" entrance with the hostess, the woman rushed on into Carol's home to impress others attending the event.

Using Humor and Positive Interactions

Another component for shaping a memorable personal style is your ability to use humor advantageously. Having a sense of humor is a definite asset. Being able to use it effectively and appropriately is a God-given talent. Humor can be used to diffuse a tense situation or ease stress in a crisis. You can use humor to illustrate or emphasize a point. Humor is a coping mechanism to aid in difficult or challenging situations. Humor allows you and others to take control over one aspect of the situation and your life—how you respond to difficult or challenging situations. If you feel totally overwhelmed or uncertain about what or how to manage the next issue, using humor may just be the right answer. Humor is good medicine, and it can help to increase productivity in your work arena.

Clever speakers often begin a presentation with a story that describes a mistake they've made or an experience in an awkward situation. While you may be fearful of incorporating humor into presentations or office projects, well-executed humor can be most powerful and memorable. For example, a sophisticated bank president laughingly tells how humbled she was when while in Japan waiting disdainfully for her limousine, she was approached by a tour group who thought she was the tour guide. Among other things, her good use of humor demonstrates to colleagues and friends that she has a sense of perspective and is comfortable with herself, the situation, and her position in life. Humor can really help to ease a tense situation. It can move listeners into a new way of thinking or help the speaker create a meaningful (and memorable) connection with them. If your listeners laugh with you, they will be more receptive to hearing the information you present, even though it opposes their thinking.

Using humor effectively and in a positive way will add to your memorable image. However, one must be careful with it. When incorporating humor, use it to make fun of a situation rather than a person or ethnic group. As with the bank president above, people will laugh because they can identify with the situation she described. It is better to make fun of yourself, to tell a funny story showing your humanness, rather than making a humorous (negative?) comment about someone else.

Even more important than a sense of humor, a memorable style depends on how well you manage the patterns of your interactions with family, co-workers, and friends. Managing the patterns of your interactions speaks to the integration of the three characteristics of style: ethical style, physical style, and social style. No one is perfect, so we all make mistakes, say something thoughtless, get angry, or fail to say thank you or I'm sorry. However, the patterns of our interactions over time tell the real story about us. If the patterns of your behavior are positive, they will reinforce the memorable image you seek. If the patterns of your behavior are negative, you must work on making the changes that are needed to create the positive, unforgettable image you desire.

Your attitudes and behaviors tell others a great deal about the kind of person you are. Whether you know it or not, your image is always on the line. An angry reaction to the clerk at the rental car station may be overheard by colleagues or, worse yet, an important client you wish to impress. People will use the behavior you display when you are "offstage" to make judgments about your core personality and who you really are, and rightfully so.

For both men and women, attitudes and behaviors toward clerical and subordinate staff, store clerks, and waiters clearly label us in a memorable way. To dispel this image, we must change our behaviors. For example, we may believe that women do not like each other or that men do not express emotions about their feelings. Our behavior and the way we treat others serves to reinforce or deny this thinking. Men define who they are by what they do, while women define who they are by how they act. Cool, aloof behaviors directed toward others often establish a negative impression about us. Men and women who are unkind, condescending, patronizing, or insensitive may quickly earn a reputation of being sexist and non-supportive. Once we have established such a reputation, people will selectively "see" just those aspects of our behavior.

What this all comes down to is how well you sell yourself and your ideas over time. Good style is not something you turn on in a meeting with top management or your favorite friends at the end of the day, but disregard with secretaries, subordinates, or acquaintances who you do not believe merit the favor of your grace and charm. To create and maintain a memorable image, good style is a major component that is absolutely essential every day in all situations. False kindness or affected reactions are transparent to those we interact with.

Defining Your Desired Image
So how do you want to be remembered? What do you need to do differently to be perceived as extraordinary and to create a memorable and unforgettable

impression? If you could be described by others in any way you choose, what are the attributes, characteristics, or traits for which you want to be known? One key to creating a new image it that you must first identify and define your desired image. The list of attributes below will help you begin this identification process. Thoughtfully consider each attribute and its definition, and then choose the five attributes or characteristics you most want to have associated with your personal and professional image.

Remember, the image you want must present a consistent pattern over all situations, every day, with every person. You cannot act one way at work and another way at a party, at home, or when serving on a committee. The STAR Approach is based on successful reinforcement of your strengths and attributes. That means reinforcement of your positive attributes to everyone around you, all of the time, every day.

A number of attributes are listed below. Review the list of attributes that follow. Then, choose the five attributes you most want to have associated with your personal and professional image.

ATTRIBUTE CHOICES

Loyal	Frugal	Informed	Cheerful
Innovative	Dependable	Self-directed	Efficient
Intelligent	Caring	Admired	Dynamic
Decisive	Reliable	Courteous	Resourceful
Creative	Team Player	Effective	Happy
Thorough	Humble	Vibrant	Respected

Humorous	Interesting	Honest	Credible
Organized	Charismatic	Thoughtful	Competent
Forceful	Understanding	Analytical	Dedicated
Sensitive	Powerful	Healthy	Exciting
Ambitious	Supportive	Articulate	Responsive
Capable	Resilient	Open-minded	Joyful
Good Manager	Conscientious	Practical	Enthusiastic
Trustworthy	Compassionate	Responsible	Optimistic

List your five choices here: _____

_____

_____

_____

_____

Now, to learn where you stand between your desired image and the perception of your present image, compare the list of attributes or characteristics you identified in Chapter One with the second list you just made using the Attribute Choices list.

Identified Attributes/ Characteristics

Desired Attributes/ Characteristics

_____   _____

_____   _____

_____   _____

_____   _____

_____   _____

If you have been honest with yourself and the attributes are the same, you have apparently established the image you desire. Now, all you have to do is keep that image intact and enhance it. However, if the attributes on the two lists are different, and you strongly desire an image that includes the characteristics identified on your second list, it's time for change.

Reread the beginning pages of this chapter on image identification, and thoughtfully consider (and possibly rewrite) the answers to the questions asked. Remember, your success with the changes you wish to make is tied directly to your ability and willingness to do the following:

1) Clearly identify and define the image you desire

2) Create a vivid and compelling picture in your mind of this image—this new you

3) Develop a plan of action to adopt the changes necessary to create your new image

4) Implement the plan and live it, every day, everywhere, all the time with everyone

This leads us to the second part of the process to develop the memorable image you seek.

Step Two: A Plan for Action
Being memorable and positively unforgettable requires a plan and a personal commitment to implement it in a disciplined manner. Adoption of your plan must become

your quest every minute of every day, until it becomes a part of your natural way of thinking, feeling, and being.

One of the more exciting mental processes with which we are blessed is the process of positive thinking. Research has demonstrated that constant reinforcement of positive thoughts and attitudes will eliminate and replace negative ones. Simply by repeating over and over, by reaffirming positive thoughts and attitudes, you can change your perception of your situation. You can change our life! Now, you are probably thinking, "Wow! This sounds like a fairly simple task—just think positive thoughts, about everything, all of the time, and my life will be terrific!"

But where do we begin? Ask yourself: What is the most significant change that I need or want to make? Why do I need or want to make this change?

Undoubtedly, your next thought will be, "Oh great! This is one of those marvelously simple things to do that is almost impossible to accomplish!"

Well, yes and no. This is a task that certainly can be accomplished. However, as we noted earlier, it will take commitment and persistence on your part. As Napoleon Hill, the renowned motivator and business consultant once said: "You don't get something for nothing."

The good news here is two-part. First, although this task will be challenging, with the STAR Approach, it is possible. Anyone willing to put forth the effort can change and create a positive, memorable image. The second part of the good news is once accomplished, you will love the results!

Using the STAR Approach, your plan of action needs to begin with an assessment of your existing attributes and special skills. Specific steps to help you reach your objective should be outlined in your action plan. Your action plan needs to include several activities that emphasize or highlight the positive attributes that will create or reinforce the image you desire. For best results, a cause and outcome model for continuous personal improvement may be useful.

Take a piece of paper and make two columns on it. Label the first column, as below, *Existing Positive Attributes* (characteristics and behaviors); the second column can be titled *Desired Positive Attributes* (characteristics and behaviors).

ATTRIBUTE COMPARISONS

Column One	Column Two
Existing Positive Attributes	**Desired Positive Attributes**
_____	_____
_____	_____
_____	_____
_____	_____
_____	_____

Now look at the list you made in Chapter One, the list of attributes that describe how you believe others presently see you. Write the positive behavioral attributes or characteristics that you noted on that list under the first column (existing positive attributes). Thinking about your current behaviors, add the other positive attributes and characteristics you have that you wish to keep and strengthen.

Under the second column, write the words shown on your second list—the list of desired attributes for which you want to be known and remembered as identified in the Attribute Choices list. Now, evaluate and assess your goal, adding to the second list other characteristics or attributes you desire that are missing or need to be strengthened or further developed. A word of caution, don't get carried away with these lists. Carefully identify the image you desire, and define it with only five to seven key words describing the positive characteristics or attributes that will establish your desired image.

Another key for developing the memorable, unforgettable image you seek requires that you find a balance between your desired attributes and what works for you—in your company, your profession, and your life. For example, if you are a CIA agent, a desire to be perceived as open and straightforward is probably not a good choice, since the behaviors inherent in your profession almost certainly preclude these attributes or characteristics being associated with you. Or if you are a lawyer or an administrative assistant to the CEO, you can't be so disorganized that it takes three days to find the client's file.

One way to understand and determine the best balance for you is to closely observe people whom you admire, who are on their way up, or who are effective leaders. You may wish to consider people involved with professional organizations or groups with which you are associated. Why is someone recognized as a leader or singled out as an important person to know or be involved with? What does this person say or do that creates a positive, memorable impression? In ten years, will you still feel the way you do today about this person?

What does this individual do that gives her respect and authority? What is the image projected by this particular individual? Why is one particular person considered a rising star? What does this person do that sets him or her apart? What makes this individual memorable in business or community activities? What are the attributes or positive characteristics you associate with the people you admire or wish to emulate?

If you will take the time to observe the people you most admire, you will find that it is more than good performance that gives these individuals positive recognition and makes them memorable. It is the combination of performance, confidence, self-esteem, and a positive attitude that blends together and flows from an internal source that knows who they are and where they are going. This combination creates an extraordinary, memorable, unforgettable personality— someone you admire, you enjoy, and most significantly, you remember.

Improvement Action Plan

The next part of the process is to identify the behaviors or actions that will work to create and reinforce the attributes or characteristics of your desired image. Use the two columns that you completed earlier in this chapter showing your existing attributes and characteristics compared with the ones you desire. Begin by identifying and listing three behaviors or activities for each word on each list that you can incorporate into your daily activities. Each of the three behaviors or activities must work to create or reinforce the positive memorable and unforgettable image you seek to create. A sample "Improvement Action Plan" is shown with a list of mentors or models that may help to inspire you.

SAMPLE IMPROVEMENT ACTION PLAN

Existing and Desired Attributes	Action or Behavior to Reinforce Or Create this Image	Mentor or Model
1) **Thoughtful**	1) Pause and think before responding to a question or giving an opinion 2) Speak more slowly 3) Listen more attentively	Al Gore Rudy Giuliani Elizabeth Edwards Bill Richardson Jackie Kennedy Suze Orman Colin Powell
2) **Articulate**	1) Use a dictionary so that the words you speak or write are correct 2) Incorporate a new word into your vocabulary each week 3) Join Toast Masters or a similar group to improve your speaking abilities	Dale Carnegie Barack Obama Rick Sanchez Ben Nighthorse Campbell Diane Sawyer Queen Noor Peter Jennings
3) **Interesting**	1) Stay current with local, national and international news – read the daily paper and weekly news magazines 2) Once a month, attend a lecture on a topic about which you know little; visit an art gallery or attend a play 3) Read two books each month, join a book discussion club, if none exists, start one	Graham Greene Oprah Winfrey Mother Teresa Cher Apolo Anton Ohno Devon Aoki Tiger Woods

The final part of the process to develop your action plan is to determine how to make the transition from your present image to your new desired image. Although this may seem to have little benefit, it is recommended that you mentally create one or more situations where you apply the behaviors or incorporate the actions that will create or reinforce your desired image. Think through, visualize, and map out each scenario. Think about situations at work, at home, or in social settings where these new behaviors or actions can be adopted or included.

How will I act if...? What will I say if ...? Be careful not to define a situation to the extreme or overemphasize possible outcomes, thereby overreacting and damaging a relationship.

Your success will be greater and come quicker if you will write out key behaviors, words, and actions, along with a few notes on how you can use these activities within the situations you have imagined. Include as many scenarios as possible. Put yourself in your home, at your desk, in church, at meetings, in the grocery store, exercise class, soccer/football/hockey game, or department store. "What will I say/do if ...?" "How will I respond if ...?"

Step Three: Perspectives for Implementing Your Action Plan
The Third Step in creating a new image or enhancing your present one involves thoughtful implementation of your plan and the behaviors and activities that create a memorable impression.

The STAR Approach relies on success through reinforcement of positive attributes. Begin now to use the STAR Approach to implement your plan of action. Simply begin at once: at home, at work, or at play to put into practice the behaviors and actions that will reinforce and emphasize your positive attributes. Don't wait until "everything" is ready to begin. "Everything" will never be ready, and you will never begin—nor finish, for that matter.

Another tip for success: keep your goals and your action plan to yourself. You may wish to discuss your goals with a close friend or mentor, but you do not need to tell everyone you see and meet what you are doing. In fact, one of the most rewarding aspects you'll derive from your new image is feedback as others notice or perceive changes without any preannouncement.

Perhaps the most complex aspect involved in changing your image is modifying your behavior. For any of us, to change our behavior takes time—time to decide what to do and time to make the adjustments. Change of any kind is not an event. Change is not something that we do, and once done, it is complete. Change is a process that goes on and on, and up and down. That is why even when you are thinking positively and adopting new behaviors, you sometimes forget and revert back to old habits. This is not a mistake. It is normal, it is learning, and it is all part of the transformation process. Remember, with the STAR Approach, you are focusing on success through the reinforcement of your positive attributes.

As noted in the first chapter, I had a significant experience that provoked a change in my behavior. You may recall my encounter with the store clerk who confronted me and asked if I wasn't the "woman who gives those talks on how to be positive and memorable." What an opportunity dumped right in my lap! Because of that interaction, I have spent the past many years working to change my behavior with not only clerks in a store, but with all other individuals with whom I come in contact. Guess what? I've learned that by being positive and responding in a more interested and caring manner, I almost always get a positive response back... and sometimes more assistance than I even asked for from the person.

Making behavioral change takes lots of time and genuine commitment to change what may seem to be even small and minor infractions. In addition to my changed behavior, another point of reward—recently a wonderful person with whom I spend much time told me that because of my interactions and behaviors with clerks and others, he was changing how he behaved with them, too. The STAR approach really does work!

Making Mistakes: Part of Learning and Growing

Since we are not perfect, we all make mistakes and react inappropriately at times. What do you do when you realize you have committed this error? The single most important thing you can do, when you have not handled a situation well, is to put aside your pride and quickly fix the situation. You must be willing to go back and say, "I am sorry—I made a mistake." Let the other person know that you want to change the outcome and remedy the situation.

Before you meet with this other person, take advantage of the situation to think about how you will incorporate the new behaviors you are adopting to create your new image. Take the time to visualize the scenario and your meeting with this person. What will you say? How will you say it? How will you act and react to the other person's responses? Saying you are sorry may not make everything okay, but it almost always improves the situation. It changes the emotional tension. It will also make both you and the other person feel better, even though the other person may not respond as positively as you wish during your conversation.

There are three things you can do to help turn around a negative situation:

1) Say you are sorry and ask the other person to forgive your transgression.

2) Thank God for giving you the insight to see your mistake and for your ability and willingness to fix it.

3) Tell yourself that you're okay—you're doing a good job, and resolve to do even better in the future.

Overnight Transformation

Another point to keep in mind: just because you have identified a new image and developed an action plan to achieve does not mean an overnight transformation will occur. You cannot be a grumble-butt one day and cinderfairy the next day. You will forget, lose your composure, and overreact to some trivial situations. We all do. Under stress or when fatigued, we tend to fall back to old habits and behaviors. Until we have fully established and adopted a new repertoire, our success with behavioral change will be intermittent. Don't be discouraged if you fall back and use an old behavior. Just keep making the changes and reinforce your positive attributes and behaviors. Believe in yourself and your capabilities—success through reinforcement of the positives!

To establish a positive, memorable image, you must refocus your past efforts. Through the reinforcement of positive attributes, the STAR Approach provides the tools you need to create your new image. You must heighten your awareness of what it means to think, feel, and behave as an extraordinary human being—a person possessed with a clear vision of what is possible and the expectations and confidence to go after and achieve your new goal.

Remember, you can have the image you desire. You can be a memorable, extraordinary person! Yes, you can! Yes, you can! Yes, you can!!!

SUMMARY THOUGHTS FROM CHAPTER TWO

1) Decide on the image you want: How do you want to be remembered?

    1)   Clearly identify and define the image you desire.

    2)   Create a vivid and compelling picture in your mind of this image—this new you.

    3)   Develop a plan of action to adopt the changes necessary to create your new image.

    4)   Implement the plan and live it, every day, everywhere, all the time with everyone.

2) Redefine your personal image.

    1)   *Ethical Style:* Define your values and identify the principles by which you live.

    2)   *Physical* Style: Speak with knowledge and authority; listen with attention and respect; be prepared and on time. Be open and positive in your approach.

    3)   *Social* Style: Social style is reflected in the way we interact with others and defined by the incorporation of "unrestrained goodwill" in our lives.

3) Good style is not something you turn on and off, depending on the people you wish to impress.

4) A sense of humor is an invaluable asset, and the ability to use it effectively and appropriately is a God-given talent.

5) Turn around the negatives.

    1)   Say you are sorry, and ask the other person to forgive your transgression.

    2)   Thank God for giving you the insight to see your mistake and for your ability and willingness to fix it.

    3)   Tell yourself that you're okay—you're doing a good job, and resolve to do even better in the future.

CHAPTER THREE

UNLOCKING YOUR POTENTIAL
FOR GOOD CHARACTER

Being a memorable person means more than simply acting out a positive image. While at the outset, "acting" positive may be a way to change your behavior, over a period of time you must assume and adopt traits and attributes that support a higher standard of behaviors.

If a positive image was all that was necessary to be positively unforgettable, more people would fall into that "extraordinary" category. Recall the definition of memorable, to be deserving or worthy of being remembered. Being unforgettable has to do with our lives, our work, our children, and our death. Thus, to be worthy of being remembered requires a commitment to a higher standard in terms of the way we live and behave.

Being memorable doesn't come without a price. Not only must you work to adopt new attributes and highlight your strengths, but you must also modify your behaviors to be consistent with and accentuate the image you desire. Being memorable seems to carry with it a demand for a certain goodness of character—a caring for and about others, and a respect for not only ourselves, but society at large.

However, this picture does not always seem be true. Certainly we've all met and seen public figures who maintained a certain element of memorableness or notoriety. Without taking anything from these individuals, at times, some of them did not seem worthy or deserving of being positively remembered. In essence, you must consider the consistency of your behaviors or patterns over time, whether you are in or out of the public eye. These behaviors and patterns are the key telling points or the reality of your ability to create a positive memorable image.

Character Defined as Memorable

As noted earlier, no one is perfect, and we all make mistakes, but often, the way we respond to a simple situation or a complex crisis signals the strength of our character. Our response must exemplify the response of an extraordinary person.

One favorite memory is of a close high school friend, Janie, who had purchased a new pair of shoes. After wearing the shoes for less than a week, they began to separate at the soles. Janie asked me to accompany her to the store to return the shoes. At the store, an attractive young man quickly waited on her. Like many teenagers, she immediately lost her confidence as she eyed the good-looking young salesman. He asked why she was returning the shoes. Janie blushed as she said, "They are palling a fart. I mean, they are palling a fart." Mortified, she became ashen in color and quiet. The young salesman smiled and said, "Goodness! So, they've fallen apart." Janie shook her head and returned the smile in appreciation for not having to repeat the statement again. The shoes were quickly exchanged, and we were on our way, laughing hysterically at what had happened.

The young man, who was not much older than us, quickly recognized how uncomfortable the statement had made Janie, and graciously helped her out of the verbal hole that she was digging. This was a spectacular example of the salesman not finding fault with error, but instead helping to pass over it as if it had not occurred. Frequently, we find ourselves having either made an error or working with someone who is stumbling to correct a misstatement. The gracious way to do this is to pass over it and move on, causing as little attention as possible.

We have all experienced that desire to crawl into a hole after making a faux pas or gaffe. Rather than emphasizing another's mistake, make it apparent that you recognize that we all make mistakes and offer acceptance and forgiveness. If you have made the blunder, take responsibility and either have a good laugh or, if appropriate, apologize. There is nothing as awkward as a verbal slip-up or social blunder where no one is willing to accept responsibility and bring closure, thus resulting in a struggle that is shared with everyone.

For each of us, our lives are filled with many opportunities. Yet we often let reckless behavior or momentary whims influence our decisions. Then, not only is the opportunity lost or diminished, but we must live with the consequences. Difficulties may certainly build character, but so does the pursuit of a dream. One key in identifying your desired image is that you have to thoughtfully and honestly evaluate your present image and the behaviors that helped you create this image. This evaluation will also cause you to assess the principles and values by which you live.

How do your values influence your behavior and important decisions? What are the principles by which you live? Are you a virtuous person? What you think, believe, and act upon with regard to each of these qualities constitutes the standards that define you and by which you live.

Principles, Values and Virtue

The difference between principles, values, and virtue is worth noting. Webster defines a *principle* as "a rule or code of conduct." Principles, then, are the unspoken rules or codes by which we live. Principles are really more of a framework for our lives—a framework that gives strength and definition to our character. Principles shape and mold our behaviors and our attitudes.

Webster defines *virtue* as "a conformity to a standard of right," a moral excellence. Virtue is also defined as a "beneficial quality" or "the power" of a thing.

Aristotle identified four characteristics to define virtue: prudence, justice, fortitude, and temperance. In a 1996 *Newsweek* magazine article, Kenneth Woodward stated, "Prudence is not cautious calculation, but practical wisdom, recognizing and making the right choice in specific situations." He went on to define *justice* as fairness, honesty, and lawfulness, *fortitude* as the strength of mind and courage to persevere in the face of adversity, and *temperance* as self-discipline, the controlling of all unruly human passions and appetites. To be virtuous then is to be a person of good character, someone who applies higher standards to the way he or she conducts his or her life. Such behavior will undoubtedly characterize an unforgettable and memorable individual.

Unlike virtues and principles, a value is the "relative worth or importance" that we give to something—the "degree of excellence" that we as individuals place on a particular object, skill, or trait. Values are, in effect, a ranking system for the good or worth that you place upon a particular object, behavior, characteristic, skill, or trait.

It seems that virtues and values are often confused. We talk of having high values when in essence what we mean are high virtues or high standards. If you are virtuous, it is a given that your values, the importance you place on things, will also be high or good. As Woodward notes, virtue is a quality of character by which an individual habitually recognizes and does the right thing.

In *The Moral Choice*, by Daniel Maguire, he states that character is the embodiment of a person's moral orientation. Maguire goes on to say that one's character reflects the roots and the moral center of the personality. He notes that "character involves the direction of a person established over the long haul." Character is defined as the consistency of patterns shown in an individual's behavior over time. The distribution of someone's positive attributes is often obvious when his or her moral orientation is observed or assessed.

Conscience must also factor into the discussion of these elements. Your conscience often acts as a barometer, indicating whether you believe your behavior is "good" or "bad." Your conscience is based upon or grounded in the principles and virtues that define your life. Your conscience is closely linked with character and reflects the moral orientation that guides you through your experiences in life.

At times, you may speak of doing something "in good conscience" or of having "a guilty conscience." Maguire says that the "principles which condition the moral self also condition the reaction of conscience." Thus, if your principles are poorly defined, your conscience is unlikely to be well developed or skilled in making decisions or judgments about "the right thing to do." The result of negative behavior without feeling or concern is what is often described as "antisocial behavior." Whereas, for the individual with well-defined principles and conscience, the result of not doing what one knows or believes to be right is a guilty conscience, a painful, nagging remorse.

Do you listen to your conscience in order to create a positive, memorable image? If you expect to be memorable, you must accept the responsibility of being conscientious, virtuous, and principled in the way you conduct your life. In order to be positively unforgettable, you must be virtuous and conscientious—not a prude, not a saint, but a person of essential good character—an extraordinary individual.

How do you measure up? Do the five attributes by which you wish to be known and remembered support and help you strengthen your character? Do your principles, virtues, and values reinforce the image you desire that will enhance your memorableness?

Just as you can use the STAR Approach to strengthen our positive attributes, you can apply this approach to develop your virtues and principles. More specifically, when you identify the image by which you wish to be remembered, you can evaluate how you are performing under these criteria. Ask yourself, do the attributes that reinforce my desired image highlight and strengthen the principles and virtues by which I live or wish to live my life?

Are there positive attributes that you have not considered that will reinforce the image of a virtuous or principled character? Using the STAR Approach to evaluate, consider if the following attributes are part of your desired image.

ATTRIBUTES EXHIBITING VIRTUOUS OR PRINCIPLED CHARACTER

- fair
- law-abiding
- honest
- integrity

- moral excellence
- fortitude
- perseverant
- courageous

- wisdom
- compassionate
- rightful behavior
- balanced
- self-disciplined
- soberness
- circumspect
- vigilant
- brave
- watchful
- fearless
- gallant
- intrepid
- stalwart
- responsible
- reasonable

Are any of these attributes likely to be used if someone who knows you well speaks about you to others? If so, list the three attributes that you believe will be associated with your name:

_____

_____

_____

Now, review the list of attributes above, and list the three attributes you most desire to be associated with your name or mentioned when you are described:

_____

_____

_____

You can use the STAR Approach and the process for adopting the approach that was described in Chapter Two. You can begin by developing an action plan to modify your behavior that will highlight and strengthen the attributes that reflect the principles and virtues you now possess and the ones you wish to acquire.

I recall working with a most talented employee, Sandra, whose reactions were at times inappropriate. During meetings or difficult conversations, Sandra was frequently smiling or giggling. Many times, this behavior was annoying and because of its inappropriateness also confusing to others and to me. At times, I would often respond angrily to Sandra. After talking with Sandra about her behavior, we both began paying close attention to the time and occasion for her reactions. We discovered that Sandra often felt nervous, unsure, and awkward in many situations. Instead of laughing, Sandra solemnly told of her fears and scares because she was uncertain about what to do or say, especially if the conversation was confrontational. Since she did not want to offend anyone, smiling or giggling was her reaction to protect herself, especially if challenged with a difficult conversation or if I or other co-workers reacted with annoyance or anger. Working with Sandra helped me become a better team player and helped Sandra participate more effectively with support from her co-workers.

Here's an example for including positive change into your life. Work on a project with someone at your office who you do not particularly like. Find ways to hear what he or she has to say; look at him when he is speaking and ask questions and agree with her ideas. At times, you may make a decision about a proposed project or idea based not on the merits of the project, but rather on your feelings about the person proposing the project or idea. I am not asking you to marry this person. I'm asking you to be a positive support person who works for the good of the department or company regardless of your personal feelings. Another point, often the characteristics, traits, or habits that we dislike in others reflect our own behaviors. Don't throw stones.....

Generosity of Spirit

As often stated, the 1980s constituted a decade of greed in our society, coupled with a "me-first" attitude. With the advent of the 1990s, society at large moved in a different direction—a direction where excessive behavior and lifestyles were not only looked upon with disfavor, but considered somewhat immoral. Companies, as well as individuals, cut back and redefined priorities. In the 90s, people wanted to connect with other human beings, with their families, or with their business. This changed behavior is continuing in the new century with greater emphasis on family life and volunteerism.

In our lives, because we often have so much, it is, at times, difficult to clarify what constitutes excess from what is a deficiency. However, virtuous behavior lends itself to a balance in one's life. Virtuous behavior seems to eliminate both excess and a lack or limitation.

We no longer judge someone to be successful just because he or she has lots of stuff. Rather, we look to the merit of the individual's (or the company's) work or actions and assess the contribution given in return to the community or to people who are less fortunate. We are evaluating the "goodness of character" within the individual or the company. As Aristotle wrote about virtue of character, "... having the right feeling, at the right time, about the right thing, toward the right people, for the right end, and in the right way is the best condition for virtue."

But then you say, "Wait a minute. I've worked really hard for this position or to make my business solid and successful, and no one's helped me." *Au, contraire.* Even though you did work very hard and sweated long hours, if you honestly evaluate the situation, you'll recognize that many others, including a Higher Power, helped you accomplish your goals and reach the level of success you have now achieved. Without your co-workers, your family and friends, without unrestrained goodwill from above, you probably wouldn't have made it to where you are. So it seems only fair that each of us gives something back. Ahhhhh.......the right thing to do.

The attributes of generosity and giving contribute substantially to the creation of a memorable image. In order to become a positive memorable individual, you must learn to foster a generosity of spirit—a giving of one's self. Often we focus more on getting or on what we will receive in return. Yet all of us have learned from experience and observation that unconditional giving often brings the biggest and the best rewards. Recall your list of desired attributes and find ways to apply them in "giving" situations.

Even if you begin giving simply to foster a memorable image, that's okay. As Suze Orman says in her book *The 9 Steps to Financial Freedom*, "Giving to say please and giving to say thank you is vital. It is the impulse to give that puts you in touch with the best part of yourself and the principles of abundance that are alive in the world.... True giving comes as an impulse, so the amount need not be cast in stone, and it may vary from month to month. All that matters is that the amount be meaningful to you and that it be given with thought, humility and gratitude."

The point is to begin—to begin to give to others. There are a number of ways to give of oneself—ways that do not cost in terms of actual dollars or material possessions. The following are some of the ways you can give to others:

- Your time

- Your ideas and creativity

- Your support or assistance

- Your praise or compliments

- Your commitment to a person or project

- Your acceptance and love

Self Evaluation

Think about your behavior last week. How memorable or unforgettable was it in terms of unconditional giving? Where, not for one nanosecond, did you think of getting something back in return. You didn't listen attentively to the pompous businessman on the airplane because he is on the board of a company for which you hope to do business. Or, did you help a co-worker with a project so she will feel obligated to help you next week, or give the boss a compliment hoping that he or she will think you are wonderful or a better person than your co-workers?

How many times did you give of yourself to others, with no regard for the outcome? How often did you give something of yourself, just to be giving, because in doing so you wanted to give pleasure or support to others?

List the five ways that you gave of yourself in a completely unconditional way during the past week.

Person	Your Action
_____	_____
_____	_____
_____	_____
_____	_____
_____	_____

Having trouble completing this assignment? Okay, then think back two weeks or maybe even a month. Can you identify five times when you gave unconditionally to someone who came into your life with no thoughts of getting something back in return?

Want some examples?

1) Your mother is old and in a nursing home. You call to tell her you are thinking of her and that you love her.

2) You say hello to, and open the door for a woman you do not know who works in your office building. This woman is not a Farrah Fawcett look-alike. She's overweight, slightly unkempt, and often unsmiling.

3) You tell your son (or daughter) how wonderful you think he (or she) is, and how happy you are that he (or she) is in your life—just because.

4) You compliment a woman or a man, whom you have never seen before and will never see again, on her colorful dress or his flashy tie as you pass in the hallway or at the airport.

5) You write a congratulatory note to the author of a fine editorial. The letter will not be published, and you do not know the author, but you simply believe the editorial deserves acknowledgment and recognition.

It is really amazing that so much of what you do "just to be nice" supports a secret agenda in your mind. In this case, "being nice" is an easy application of the STAR Approach. Does that make the outcome wrong or lacking in value? Indeed not! But this exercise is part of the introspection you need to complete in order to become a more memorable person...a positively unforgettable person.

This thinking is not to say nor imply that it is wrong to give to others or do something with the hope or anticipation of receiving something in return. That's real life. Much of what you give to others is done with the hope or expectation of receiving some payback. The question to ask and ponder is how likely are you to give of yourself if there is no possibility of personal gain?

Do you know someone who does make a practice of unconditional giving of self? Does her or his behavior make the person more memorable? In all likelihood, the response is yes.

One person who comes to mind is a great SalPal, a most extraordinary woman! This grand eighty-nine-year-old person *always* has the time to see you, listen to your concerns or glee, and share ideas for helping you resolve troubling issues and see ways to expand your options. Over the past fifty years, Sally has helped a zillion people of all ages. She is truly one of the most giving people I have ever known. I have seen Sally give with no expectation of getting anything ever in return. Often if you admire a piece of jewelry or an art object in her home, she will pick it up, hand it to you and say, "Take it home with you." What an amazing example of unconditional caring and generosity of spirit! What a marvelous role model.....I want to be like her!!!

Using the same process developed in Chapter Two; create a plan of action to help identify ways that you can give of yourself—small acts of unconditional giving. To help you get started, a simple action plan for unconditional giving follows.

SAMPLE PLAN FOR UNCONDITIONAL GIVING

Person	Your Gift
Your Mom, Dad, sister, brother	A phone call or card, "just want to say I love you."
The mechanic who worked diligently on your car last week	A thank you note for a job done well.
The owner of a restaurant you used to frequent when you worked in the neighborhood	You don't have time for lunch, but you're nearby. So you stop, dash in and tell Harold hello and how much you miss the great lunches at his restaurant.
An older neighbor whose lovely garden you notice and admire each summer day	A note on her door telling her how much you enjoy seeing her garden; Or in January, deliver a small bouquet with a note telling her you're looking forward to seeing her garden in July.
Any one	A helping hand with a door, a warm smile and a pleasant "good morning" or an offer to help with the next project in the office.

Selective Giving

Just as you have made the decision to develop a memorable image and become a memorable person, thought is required to know when and what to give of yourself. Although each of us has much to give, our time and resources are often limited. Even though spontaneous giving is always good, giving of oneself is not necessarily helpful or beneficial if it depletes your reservoir of resources. I am referencing the giving of our time or energy to an event, organization, or person, while failing to reserve the resources or the time necessary to give to a cause or person(s) where a need exists and the benefit is greater.

Often you give so much to your business and community that you have little or no time for your family. Or you give to the community and your friends, while overlooking your co-workers and those who have helped you accomplish great things. Family members, co-workers, and friends who have supported you are often taken for granted. So when you finally get around to them, you are too tired to give or have no time to give. Thus, while others may view you as memorable, those who are the most important in your life have a very different opinion of your worthiness for being remembered positively.

In order to use your time and energy well, you must be selective when giving of yourself and your time. Being selective means that some of the giving you provide must be conditional, and that the return on your investment of time and energy is beneficial in some way to you. Selective giving will not prevent you from giving many unconditional gifts of yourself throughout the day. Rather, selective giving will help you prioritize, thereby making you a better giver through better use of your resources and your time.

This point is illustrated by a passage from Stephen Covey's book *First Things First*. In his book, Covey says, "Consider the big picture—what you care about, what makes the moments in your life meaningful. The key in this connection lies in the clarity of your vision around such questions:

- What's most important?

- What gives your life meaning?

- What do you want to be and do in your life?"

Impartial Receiving

Actually many of us strive to be great givers, and in many ways we are. However, some of us fail to recognize that the acceptance of gifts from others is another form of giving. Why is it that some people want to give to others, but are unwilling to receive? Do you have a false notion that you are virtuous if you are a martyr? Hence, "Oh, I don't deserve that" or "you just take that right home and keep it for yourself" or "thanks for saying I look pretty, but my hair is a mess" or "oh no, not with this wrinkled shirt."

Acceptance of gifts also includes the ability to graciously accept compliments. Compliments for your work, your fund-raising skills, your appearance, your finely-cooked dinner, your time as a volunteer, or your presence are gifts from another. "I love having you here with me!" "Thank you, it pleases me to have you tell me."

When you are unwilling to receive, you deny the pleasure of giving to family, friends, or colleagues. You keep a monopoly on giving behavior and, in essence, maintain an element of control over the giver and the situation. Further, you are saying to the giver that the gift, which often conveys his or her love, is not wanted. What a sad way for you to be remembered.

Learning to accept the gifts of others is in reality learning to accept gifts for yourself—believing that you are worthy and deserving of receiving a gift. If you are a great giver but a poor receiver, ask yourself who you are hurting the most when you turn away or discount the gift of another. Doesn't being a great giver also imply the giving of fun or pleasure to others? If you enjoy giving, wouldn't someone else enjoy it equally as much?

Does this behavior describe you? Are you only comfortable giving, but not comfortable receiving? Do gifts from others make you feel unworthy or uncomfortable? If so, consider further the idea that allowing others the joy of giving (to you) is a gift that only you can grant. To be memorable and unforgettable means to be responsive and receptive to others. Open your mind and your heart, and give others the opportunity of giving to you.

List below five ways you can adopt the STAR Approach and change your behavior to become a more gracious receiver and a true giver.

Giver/Gift	Your New Response
_____	_____
_____	_____
_____	_____
_____	_____
_____	_____

Now, as in Chapter Two, develop an action plan to guide your work as you incorporate success through reinforcement of attributes.

SAMPLE IMPARTIAL RECEIVING PLAN

Giver/Gift	Your New Response
Your grandfather sends a religious pamphlet from a church beyond the scope of your spiritual orientation.	Write a warm note thanking him for sending the information and acknowledge his love and concern for you.
A co-worker offers to help with a project. Even though you could use the help, you decline because you don't want to feel obligated.	You happily accept, because you need the help and you know it will make your co-worker feel good to be a part of the project.
Your daughter and son-in-law offer to take you downtown with them; but you don't "want to be a burden" so you decline and take the bus.	You beam and say "How wonderful – now I won't have to ride that silly old bus!"

SUMMARY THOUGHTS FROM CHAPTER THREE

1) **Character Counts.**
In order to be positively unforgettable, we must be virtuous and conscientious.

2) **Make Virtue a Part of Your Life.**
Incorporate the following into your life:

Practical wisdom

Fairness

Honesty and lawfulness

Perseverance in adversity

Self-discipline.

3) **Be Generous.**
> Give of your time.

> Give your thoughts and ideas.

> Give your support or volunteer assistance.

> Give your money.

> Give your praise.

> Give your commitment.

> Give others the opportunity of giving to you.

> Give your love and acceptance.

CHAPTER FOUR

UNLOCKING YOUR POTENTIAL
FOR A POSITIVE SELF-IMAGE

In order to care about others and treat them well, you must first care about yourself. When you feel good about yourself, you behave in ways that are different from the ways you act when you are "not in a good spot." Ironically, self-esteem is part of a regenerating cycle. The better you feel about yourself, the more positively you think and act. Conversely, negative feelings and thoughts cause degeneration that results in a negative attitude and negative behaviors.

When you feel good about yourself, you react and respond to others with positive, supportive behaviors. Your positive behavior reinforces your good feelings about yourself, and you experience greater success. When you do not feel good about yourself, you tend to react negatively and treat others poorly. Then, you become angry and feel guilty, and you like yourself even less than before. You fall into a cycle of disappointment and failure.

Once you recognize that your attitude can and does affect your destiny, you can turn your life around. Abraham Lincoln said, "Most people are as happy as they make up their minds to be." It's true. A positive attitude leads to a positive self-image.....and, a positive self-image is one of the most important tools necessary to create a positive, memorable image. Look again at the attributes you identified to be associated with your newly created memorable image. The essential key here for being an unforgettable person is that a positive attitude is a mandatory requirement.

Garbage In—Garbage Out

Many people believe they are victims of their environment and circumstance. We think we have to wait for luck or our karma to change in order to have a different life or lifestyle. Faulty thinking—this is simply not true. You can begin right now to change your life. A first step to making changes in your life is to recognize that you and only you control your feelings, your thoughts, and your destiny.

You are what you are, and you are where you are in your life because of the thoughts and feelings in your mind. Each of us has the power to change our destiny by changing the way we think and feel about ourselves and our lives.

Our minds function much like a computer functions. If you don't like what is happening in your life, you need to consider reprogramming the information you are putting into your mind. Finding ways to change the information through changes in the way you think will clearly affect the outcome.

In his book *Soar WithThe Eagles*, author Chuck Lauer verifies this point. He says, "… These people can take the most demoralizing circumstances and turn them into new opportunities. They have the kind of positive and winning attitude that's absolutely essential in today's healthcare environment … as well as in life. The battle cry of my industry—and yours—can no longer be 'Isn't it awful?' … we need to stare adversity in the face and proclaim, 'What an opportunity!'" What a great point Chuck is making and one that we all should enthusiastically adopt.

Positive thinking or a positive mental attitude (PMA) is a prerequisite for creating a memorable image. Once you recognize that your attitude can and does affect your destiny, you can turn your life around. A change in attitude is really a matter of expectations.

This theory may seem simplistic and unrealistic, but it works. Having a positive mental attitude has been a successful tool for countless great leaders, athletes, motivational consultants, and ordinary people. Significantly, many of these people have found that one of the most important tools for success is a positive attitude or the ability to maintain a positive approach to life even in the face of adversity.

Success in life occurs when you get what you are seeking. Success may be a thriving business, a happy marriage, a college degree, the next big sale, or making a change in your behavior. But you don't always get what you seek in life. How do you maintain a positive attitude when small things go wrong or a major crisis affects your life?

The impact of attitude on our lives is tremendous. Your attitude is vitally important to your success. It can stimulate or break your staff, your family, or yourself. You have a choice every day about the attitude that you will adopt and embrace for the day. You cannot control other people, and often you may lose control to circumstances, but you can control your attitude and your behaviors. Those two things, your attitude and your behavior, are the only things you fully and completely control. How you react and respond to negative or great experiences is based in great part on your character and your attitude about life.

Several years ago, I had a devastating and humiliating collapse in both my personal and professional life. In order to maintain my composure, I focused almost completely on my business, the hospital consulting firm. My marriage dissolved, and because of issues created by my ex-husband, I had unbelievable financial challenges with the IRS. While I did not always react positively or sometimes even appropriately with my staff (all of whom loyally stood by me), I was able to keep the consulting firm in operation. The firm continued to successfully sell and deliver marketing research services, program and facility design changes, and promotional services to rural and urban hospitals. And because of my focused energy, generally I was able to maintain a positive attitude with clients and with my staff.

Although the challenge of paying the IRS over $490,000 within six years seemed overwhelming, I had to believe in myself and believe that I could pay off the debt to the IRS, pay the salaries of my staff, and pay for the services of the accountants and attorneys helping me. And, astonishingly, with the help of my dedicated staff and others, I did make all of the payments while maintaining a positive attitude about my life.

The ability to maintain a positive attitude or a positive approach to life even in the face of adversity is difficult. Even individuals who always seem positive and outgoing have "bad" days. Days when you are tired or nothing seems to go right. Days when you just don't feel "great" or believe you can make a difference with any activity. What do you do, and how do you change this feeling? How do you change your behavior and your thinking so that you feel good about yourself and experience good results and outcomes from your activities?

Tools for Change
In order to make changes in your behavior, you must first learn how to make changes in your mind. While this effort does not require complex psychotherapy, it does require the adoption of basic skills that will change or modify your thinking. Using the STAR Approach, you will

see that reinforcement of desired attributes provides the exact tools you need to be successful. Your success rate will be proportionate to your ability to apply behavioral changes in your life.

A well-known fact states that we come to believe information that we hear repeatedly. This is the principle of autosuggestion. Thus, if you tell yourself you are doing well, looking good, or feeling great, you will do well, look good, and feel great. Conversely, if you berate yourself for making a mistake, criticize your appearance, and recite your problems to friends, you will think, feel, and act in a negative way. Often, allowing such behavior to infect your life may lead to a negative performance or outcome.

One of the most effective formulas for increasing self-confidence was first described by Napoleon Hill in the 1930s in his book *Think and Grow Rich*. Hill set out five simple principles that he believed were essential to developing and sustaining a positive mental attitude and to achieving success in life. Hill believed that if you truly wanted to accomplish a goal, you had to reach a level of "desire" in your mind—not just a want for something, a hope or a wish, but an incredibly strong feeling of compelling desire that inspires and infiltrates your very being.

To reach that level of desire in your mind, Hill recommended writing out the goal or "definite major purpose" that you wanted to accomplish. Then he suggested reading this goal aloud every morning and every evening in order to facilitate the occurrence of the event.

Principles for Change

The process Hill described can work to help you change your attitude and approach to life. Hill believed that in order to achieve a goal or definite purpose, five reasons must be established to help you succeed or accomplish your goal. My interpretations of these five reasons follow.

- I know I have the ability to achieve the object of my definite purpose. I will be persistent and work with continuous action toward its attainment.

- I realize the thoughts in my mind will eventually reproduce themselves in outward actions and physical reality. Therefore, I will eliminate all negative thoughts and messages I give myself. I will concentrate on thinking positive thoughts and on creating a clear picture of the successful person I wish to become. (The STAR Approach in action!)

- I know that through the principle of repetitious thought, the desire that I hold persistently in my mind will seek expression through some practical means. I will concentrate on repeating positive thoughts aimed at building my confidence and achieving my goals.

- I have written a description of my goal/definite purpose. I will read this description every morning and evening and work positively to attain it—to become a positively unforgettable person.

- I realize no wealth or position can endure unless it is built on truth and justice. I will engage in no activity that does not benefit all whom it affects. I will succeed by securing the cooperation of others because I believe in them and I believe in myself.

Turning Desire into Accomplishment

The establishment of a definite purpose or goal is a method for turning a desire into tangible results. According to Hill, six definite, practical steps are required in order to achieve your goal. My interpretation of these steps is outlined below.

1) Determine *exactly* what you wish to attain. You must be definitive and precise. Your goal or purpose cannot be a vague, general thought, like to make more money or close a sale. Be very specific. What do you truly want to accomplish?

2) Determine what you intend to give or do to make your goal a reality. You cannot get something (of value) for nothing. What will you do, or how will you go about accomplishing your goal?

3) Establish a definite date when you will accomplish the goal or possess the object you desire. Be realistic in determining the amount of time needed to accomplish your goal.

4) Create a plan to carry out your desire, and begin at once. Put the plan into action even if you are not fully prepared. If you wait until all conditions are exactly right or all components are in place, you won't ever begin.

5) Write out a clear, concise statement of the goal or object you desire. In your statement, name the time frame you have set, state what you will give in return, and briefly describe the plan you will use to accomplish the goal.

6) Read this statement aloud, just before bed and again in the morning. After you read the statement, take a few minutes and visualize yourself in the situation that your goal creates. See yourself getting what you seek—feel excited, positive, thrilled, blessed about receiving your goal. Allow yourself to feel exactly the way you will feel when you receive your desired goal.

In order to achieve success, Hill believed that all of the steps had to be followed or completed. Step number six is especially important. You may think it's impossible to see yourself "in possession of the money" or "receiving the promotion or award" you desire. However, visualization is an activity where desire excels over a mere wish. Creative visualization is purposeful imagining—the act of seeing your goal in your mind's eye. To achieve success, you must persist in repeating your goal twice a day, and visualize yourself in a situation with the goal accomplished.

Remember, only you can make your objective a reality. You must motivate yourself and make a commitment to achieving your goal. To establish your commitment to success, take the time to write out your goal or "definite purpose" and sign your name and date the document. Completing this activity will reinforce the importance you give to achieving your goal. Three to four times each week, read the principles that you have written until they are firmly centered in your mind.

One excellent example of someone having an ultimate goal and using a definite purpose is the amazing and successful run for the presidency conducted by Barack Obama and his campaign staff. Not only was President Obama truly focused on his goal, but he was able to reinforce this goal into the minds and activities of his campaign staff. With the assistance of his wife Michelle and his campaign staff, thousands of people around the country were motivated to work for his campaign on a local level and help him win the presidency.

Moving Forward
Learning to motivate yourself is a form of behavior modification. **YOU** are your most powerful motivator.

Instead of simply going through each day reacting to events and people, you can adopt a proactive approach to accomplish your goals. In fact, once you adopt a proactive approach, you will find that you can apply that approach to all phases of your life. This activity supports and reinforces the STAR Approach— creating success through reinforcement of your positive strengths and attributes.

Being proactive means that you will take action in order to accomplish something. Instead of waiting for something to happen and then reacting, you can "reach out" to achieve your goals. You can act first by assisting or facilitating the outcome you desire.

For example, let's say you have mailed an introductory package of information about your sales product to a potential new client. You can wait until the client sees the material and decides to call you. In this situation, you are hoping your client will take the initiative to react positively to the materials he or she received—a wait and see approach. Or you can adopt a proactive approach and can call the client to accomplish the following:

- Make certain the material was received

- Explain or discuss the material with the client to make certain he understands the concept

- Offer to come by and demonstrate the product

- Call and make a sale by telephone

To help motivate and move you, the following guidelines will lend some structure and hopefully inspiration to establish a proactive approach to life.

- Be a proactive achiever, a doer, someone who moves and gets things done.

- Don't wait until conditions are perfect to begin. Conditions will never be perfect, and waiting for the right timing or situation is a way to procrastinate.

- Plan ahead. Be prepared to remove obstacles or solve problems before they occur.

- Remember, ideas alone do not bring success. Ideas only have value if you act on them.

- Use action to reduce your fears and gain confidence. Do the things you are afraid to do, and your fears will decrease.

- Begin at once! Do not wait until the spirit moves you. Allow your enthusiasm to bubble over and excite you.

- Don't waste time getting ready by fussing with preparations. This behavior is just another form of procrastination to avoid failure or even success.

- Think in terms of now, today. If you wait for tomorrow, next week, or later, you probably will not begin. Waiting for tomorrow can be synonymous with the word "never" when we talk of accomplishing goals.

People who are successful in any business believe in themselves, and they think "I can achieve, I will succeed." Losers think of themselves as victims. Losers concentrate on what they should have done or would have done, "if only..." Losers focus on what they cannot do or what others did to them and how this action prevented their success from occurring.

Among the many books written by motivational experts, the same basic points are made and underscored in each book. These five points are critical elements when creating an unforgettable image:

- Believe in yourself (and your product and your company).

- Set high standards and well-defined goals.

- Manage your "mental environment," and avoid negative thoughts.

- Stop complaining and finding fault (people don't want to hear it).

- Your attitude about life and yourself determines how successful and happy you are.

My dear friend Kris tells a story about her grandfather who she describes as a wise and thought-provoking man. Kris says, "My grandfather would frequently challenge me with games to help me observe and appreciate my surroundings. We would walk around the desert near his humble self-made stone home, and he would share the realities of how delicately balanced the desert and all of its life sources were. He taught me to appreciate the various intricacies of nature, and to interfere as little as possible. One day in a discussion regarding faith, he asked if I found it necessary to see something in order to believe in it. At age ten, I couldn't be fooled and told him that I did. He asked how I knew something didn't exist, if I had never seen it. This concept changed my whole prospective on faith and influenced how I approach change and life. So often, life is not as we see or perceive it, but is far more complex. Events are not only as we perceive them, but also as others perceive the same event. Understanding requires us to recognize the reality of others as well as our own."

Success or Failure

So, if we know the differences between winners and losers, why do so many people fail or only go part of the way toward getting what they profess to want out of life? What are the factors or variables that make a difference for one person, but not for another? And if you know that you can get what you want by changing your attitude or your approach to life, why are you unwilling to do what is necessary to accomplish your goal?

It is astonishing to look about and see the number of people with wonderful, extraordinary talents who are miserably unhappy, in trouble with their families, running from the law, and feeling as if they have no control—no ability to make their lives different. Somewhere along the way, these people gave up control of their lives by giving up control of their attitude. A positive mental attitude really can convert the negatives and provide the mental assistance to change your behaviors.

From personal experience, I know that maintaining a positive self-image or attitude is not an easy task. It takes extra effort, perseverance, and a relentless reinforcement of positive thoughts and feelings. On some days, even the most successful people must tell themselves that they are feeling great and doing very well. On other days, everything is great, and there is no way to fail.   STAR SHINE!

Self-estimation profoundly affects your sense of personal strength and influences your behaviors. A lack of self-esteem will cause you to feel inadequate or insecure. When you feel uncertain of yourself, you tend to hold back and will not share with others. You become afraid that you will make a mistake or say something dumb, so you avoid taking the risk of really getting to know someone or of giving your opinion in a meeting or conversation. Such behaviors will keep positive excitement from occurring in your life because you avoid new or unfamiliar activities. At times, you may even prevent kindness or warmth because of your fears and insecurities.

One of my favorite motivators is Robert H. Schuller, founding pastor of the Crystal Cathedral in Garden Grove, California. In response to the question, "When will tough times start turning around?" Reverend Schuller says, "When you do." He focuses on what he calls "possibility thinking," which is the affirmative management of ideas.

Possibility thinking lets you consider all possible options to solve a problem or change your behavior. It's your attitude, remember? Problems are nothing but opportunities or stepping stones to your goals. As Norman Vincent Peale once stated, "When life gives you lemons, you make lemonade."

There are three components that make up and influence our self-esteem. Although these components are all required to achieve positive self-esteem, one of the components may be more important to you than are the other two components. Or because of circumstances, the importance of the components may change from one day to the next.

COMPONENTS OF SELF-ESTEEM

COMPONENT	IMPORTANCE
Sense of belonging	feelings of love and acceptance
Sense of worth	having value or being respected as a valuable person
Sense of competence	being recognized as a capable person

People with a positive self-image usually have several identifiable characteristics. Some of these characteristics are shown below:

- An overall perspective about their life that is positive

- A sense of humor

- An ability to make friends easily

- An ability to quickly establish rapport and relate well with others

- Acceptance of their physical appearance

- An ability to see something good in difficult or negative situations

The Good News

The good news is that positive thinking can be learned. A positive mental attitude is a key attribute of memorable people. Your attitude in life and about life determines how successful you will become and how memorable you will be. A healthy self-esteem will enable you to accept new challenges and enrich your life through long-lasting relationships with others. A healthy self-esteem maintains your self-confidence that leads to the achievement of your goals and dreams in life.

Learn to find the silver lining in difficult or negative situations. Every situation, good or bad, has positive and negative factors. If the situation is good, you see or feel only the positive factors. Conversely, if the situation is bad, you see or feel only the negative factors. See the big picture, find the good and the bad factors in every situation, and emphasize the positive factors in your mind. This is not a Pollyanna approach; rather it is a way of seeing everything differently, with a broader view. The bad factors do not disappear. But when weighed with the good factors, the bad factors have less potency and become manageable.

Here are some tips:

- Start each day with a positive thought or prayer.

- Respond positively and with enthusiasm when asked how you are. Instead of saying "I'm fine," try saying "I feel great!"

- Give yourself compliments about how you look or how well you presented information at the meeting.

Having a positive self-image makes you a more attractive individual. Being attractive does not necessarily mean that you are beautiful and perfectly proportioned or tall, handsome, and well built. One aspect of being attractive is learning the ability to make others feel special or unique. Learning to add value in your communication with another person is a quality that always leaves a positive impression. If you create or reinforce special feelings in another person, you will be remembered well. To be memorable means to be an appealing and enjoyable person. Almost all of this perception is directed by your attitude and reinforced by your behavior. A positive self-image and enthusiastic behavior create a most memorable being!

SUMMARY THOUGHTS FROM CHAPTER FOUR

1) **Recognize that YOU and only you control your feelings, your thoughts, and your destiny.**

2) **Positive thinking or a positive mental attitude is a prerequisite for creating a memorable image.**

3) **Your attitude determines your altitude or level of success in life.**

4) **Develop and draft the reasons for change in your life:**

   - I have the ability to achieve the object of my definite purpose. I will be persistent and work with continuous action toward attainment.

   - I realize the thoughts in my mind will eventually reproduce themselves in outward actions and physical reality. I will eliminate all negative thoughts and messages and think only positive thoughts.

   - I will concentrate on repeating positive thoughts, building my confidence, and achieving my goals.

   - I will write a description of my goal and will read this description every morning and evening.

   - **I will engage in no activity that does not benefit all it affects.** I will succeed by securing the cooperation of others because I believe in them, and **I believe in myself**.

5) **Motivate yourself: Be proactive. YOU are your most powerful motivator!**

6) Adopt "possibility thinking" to manage ideas and consider all options for change.

7) To be memorable and unforgettable means to be an appealing and enjoyable person. Almost all of this perception is directed by your attitude and reinforced by your behavior. A positive self-image and enthusiasm really do create a most unforgettable being!

CHAPTER FIVE

UNLOCKING YOUR POTENTIAL FOR POWER

Suppose you're one of thirty-seven vice presidents, all working hard, all scrambling, and all waiting to be recognized and noticed. What do you do to set yourself apart?

Or maybe you're one of only two or three midlevel managers, vying for the vice president's job that has just opened up. How do you distinguish yourself to get the promotion in an appropriate way without harming or possibly even promoting co-workers?

To be memorable means to have power. Although memorable individuals are almost always powerful people, powerful people are not always memorable or at the least positively memorable. Power should not be regarded as the ability to make decisions, but rather, the ability to influence or persuade others to do what needs to be done. Power without followers holds little value. Followers can participate actively, passively, or not at all. This definition brings forth the reality that active buy in or at least passive acceptance is very important to the success of the individual allotted power. We can all recall the history of kings who led successfully, were overtaken, and then were replaced or killed.

For many people, a discussion about power causes discomfort and unease. Power is often associated with manipulation, and many perceive it as a bad or negative factor. However, the manner in which power is used is more significant than the power itself. The use and misuse of power depends solely on the person who is using it. Power through people is a potent force for change and is a prerequisite for accomplishment.

Often, power is demonstrated through cooperation and compromise—a collaboration of all parties to achieve a win-win outcome.

Power or the drive for power is a strong motivator because it symbolizes a desire to affect and to influence others. Power brings with it the ability to do the following:

- Set the rules or establish how an event or activity will occur

- Make others dependent, interdependent, or independent

- Create possibilities or options for outcomes

- Help others or provide useful referrals or resources

- Influence or frustrate people who perceive that they are without power

Personal or Position Power

Personal power can increase your leadership abilities and add to your success and potential. Personal power is not an inherent trait, but it can be learned. Often we have personal power, but we don't use it to our best advantage. People who are motivated by a need for personal power are often more effective leaders. They create a higher sense of responsibility among followers and build a stronger team spirit.

Having personal power and knowing how to use it properly can create a memorable, unforgettable difference. Personal power may enhance or augment the power you have because of position or status. But even if you don't have position, status, or social power, well-polished personal power will certainly create a more memorable you. Power that is personalized can be negative if it is exploitive, self-aggrandizing, or demeaning. The extent to which you accept responsibility for your behaviors and actions equals the extent of your power. In order to be truly effective, you need to learn to use power with integrity, or you will lose more authority than you gain.

Often your position in a family, community, or organization grants you power that you can choose to accept or deny. With position, your power is derived from who you are or by your role in an organization. Although position may give authority, position does not always give power or the ability to influence or persuade others to action. Position power is rarely enough to substantiate permanent change among your colleagues, but it can be effective with subordinates, committee members, or family members.

An essential key to being memorable is that you must learn to use power thoughtfully, judiciously, and effectively. Sharing power and information rather than guarding or hiding them will enhance and develop your relationships with others. Sharing power and information gives others the opportunity to reach conclusions, solve problems, accept responsibility, and justify decisions that are made. However, sharing power and information does hold some risk. Respondents may reject, criticize, or challenge you or the information you provide. Learning how to effectively respond and relate to different people with diverse skills and needs requires wise utilization of the power that you have been granted. Thoughtful consideration of cause and effect or risk-benefit analysis must be weighed prior to the development and implementation of decisions.

When discussing information or plans for a project, it is best to begin your discussion with a smile and in a friendly way. If you present your information with a statement that supports agreement, you will encourage a positive response from others. Reaching agreement with one person will lead to agreement with others participating in the discussion. Asking stimulating questions that highlight or reinforce your point will also encourage other to think in different directions and may help move them toward your point of view.

If disagreement does occur, let the person make his point and do not interrupt. At all costs, try to avoid an argument and let your opponent make his point. You can discuss the differences in your point and his, but don't attack the person. You need to keep the discussion focused on the issue and never tell the person he is wrong—it will only escalate the situation. To change directions, you may wish to suggest other options or ways of managing the point being conversed. If it turns out that you are wrong, do admit your mistake quickly and move on with your discussion pints.

To do anything or carry out a task requires action, and action requires power. An engine cannot run without the power to act. Similarly, a person cannot function effectively without the ability to act. Different kinds of engines require different types of power sources. Some engines run on diesel fuel, some use gasoline, and some use electricity. Similarly, different kinds of people require different kinds of power. You can better understand what makes an effective leader by considering the kinds of power used among effective leaders.

Even though the driver of an automobile has turned on the ignition and the motor is running, the engine will not produce its potential to move the wheels if the driver has not engaged the appropriate gear. Likewise, in an organization, even though the leader is motivated and the followers are moving toward a goal, they may not reach that goal if the leader has neglected learning how to recognize and fill the needs of followers, placing the organization in the appropriate gear to cause movement at the optimal speed and in the best direction. For each act, there is a response to fill or meet the needs of another person. Followers want to know the benefits that will be received for giving their support to the project.

Many articles and books discuss various types of power and how to achieve it, but sometimes achieving power is the easiest part. Understanding how to use power properly and without a need for ultimate control takes years of experience, both in real life and through education. Following are four of the most common descriptions of power that will help amplify your ability to lead, follow, and communicate.

Goal Power
Goal power is the power that comes when an effective leader identifies a desired outcome and clearly articulates the outcome of the goal. The leader must also recognize the options needed to achieve the goal and establish specific objectives with employees, family members, or friends. One person may become the leader simply because he or she develops an idea and helps others accomplish it. In this instance, buy in is very important to the success of the project and should be obtained from thoughtful leaders in the group. Without buy in, the project will lack momentum and may encounter frank sabotage. Conversely, if a high potential for success is attached to the goal, more people will want to become involved, and they will push for the project to succeed and become followers of the leader.

In this scenario, the mere existence of a clear accepted goal can create power for the leader. The individual has developed a reality that includes an expectation for a specific outcome to occur. This reality has power. When others (employees, friends, family) create a space in their reality with a similar expectation, the goal (power) is a mutual driving force. If others have different expectations or realities, they can become an impediment.

An example of someone with goal power is Governor Bill Richardson who has successfully focused on reducing the number of deaths in New Mexico due to accidents caused by intoxicated automobile drivers. When Richardson became governor in 2002, a primary issue for change was to reduce the number of alcohol-related traffic fatalities. In 1996, New Mexico topped the chart with the most DWI fatalities per capita in the U.S. However, after several years of numerous DWI checkpoints and the 2005 law requiring all convicted drunk drivers to have an interlock device placed in their vehicle for one year, Governor Richardson was able to announce in March 2008 that New Mexico was no longer among the top ten states with the highest level of alcohol-related traffic fatalities. New Mexico reported 135 alcohol-related fatalities in 2008, down from 177 in 2007. While the State may be off of the top ten lists, the number of alcohol-related fatalities continues to be a problem that Governor Richardson remains committed to solving.

Communication Power

Who speaks to whom? Who ignores whom? Who keeps others informed and up to date? Who keeps others in the dark? Who listens to whom? Who are the reliable sources of information? Communication comes in the form of interaction and may be a spoken word, smile, gesture or nod, a pat on the back, a rigid body, or an exit from the room.

Communication power comes from being perceived as a credible source of ideas, actions, or messages in a particular area or about an important topic or issue. Even with effective methods of communication, there are varying degrees of credibility attached to various message sources. Credible sources of communication cause people to act and react in concert. Non-credible sources may get action, but the action is often accomplished by chaos and coercing, rather than by attentive communication.

How do you communicate with influence or effective attention? How do you communicate in a positive, memorable way? Actions can communicate ideas and information, but actions do not always credibly communicate the information you wish distributed. For example, the threat of suicide communicates to the world a need for help. Yet even though this act may clearly get the message across, the act of suicide is ineffective because of its destruction to the person who communicated the message.

Most importantly, for effective and memorable communication, your message needs to be structured or composed for your listener. Often you compose a message based on what you think is significant rather than on a point that is meaningful to the person with whom you are speaking. Think about your audience. What is the best way to send information to this person? If presenting information to the financial manager, you will want to use data that demonstrates the numbers in an appropriate table or graph. And you need to avoid the use of glitzy promotional language or hand motions--it just won't fly in finance! However, if you are talking with the marketing manager, dramatize your ideas with colorful stories and promotional examples that reinforce your points.

How do you communicate, especially using e-mail, so that your message is well received and remembered positively? Thoughtful and precise communication makes the recipient comfortable and creates a desire to respond positively. Communication oriented to the listener establishes or reinforces your effectiveness as well as your conversation. Put yourself in the listener's shoes (or position). If appropriate, use empathy and view the issues or the situation from the other person's perspective.

An individual with extraordinary communication power is former president Bill Clinton. His ability to positively connect with people around the world has been recognized as a most remarkable skill and ability. Because of his consummate communication skills, Clinton is a frequent speaker at major national and international corporate meetings and gatherings.

Follower Power
Follower power is much more like popularity and is based in part on the relationship between the leader and the follower. Someone with many followers often seems to attract others without really trying to do so. A popular person may be perceived as popular for any number of good or bad reasons. But his or her popularity grows to some extent simply because others want to be associated with and connected to this person. Sometimes this increase in followers occurs for reasons as simple as the need to be associated with someone who is popular and well accepted. However, the opposite can be true, and individuals may be shunned or ignored because potential followers do not wish to be seen or associated with this person.

Does that mean that you should not stand up for issues or individuals that may be unpopular? Not necessarily. What it means is that you should evaluate and measure the level of power or influence before attempting to make significant changes in the structure of what is acceptable. The leader who has follower power often maintains leadership by offering "follower-belonging" power. Followership is based on individual objectives to meet psychological needs. By joining the leader, the follower is able to satisfy his or her needs while providing the leader with more power created by a larger number of followers.

Unconsciously, the message given by the leader to followers is "follow me and you will be in the group." Effective leaders attract followers because the leader is believable or reputable in what he or she represents. In using power, a leader gives certain powers to his or her followers. You may want to be with the "in-group" and gain recognition for your presence in this memorable group. A leader's position is maintained and grows stronger because of her followers. Leadership begins with the follower rather than with the leader, but is transferred to the leader when the number of followers is large or publicly influential.

Follower power is best exemplified by Sarah Palin. After even only a short time on the national political stage, Palin has managed to create a strong following of believers who think she is creditable and strongly support her message. Palin's position clearly seems to be maintained and enhanced because of her committed followers.

Leader Power

From a child's perspective, most of the people around us have power. Because of our position as a child, we had little or no authority with the adults in our world. Our parents, teachers, and other adults made the rules, and we followed with decisions made on our behalf.

Leadership exists only if followership is produced. As noted, leadership begins with the follower. In this situation, power comes from the relationships developed between the leader and the followers. Successful leaders are sensitive to what others perceive as appropriate behaviors or beliefs of the leader to the followers. Influential or power-oriented behavior is tempered by maturity and self-control. Successful and memorable people are comfortable using this influence to motivate and influence others.

Sometimes, leadership power is derived from physical power or position power. The leader is strongest because of his size (often a factor for tall men) or because of his or her position in an organization or firm (I'm the CEO, so I have power). Here, it is important to recognize that the art of developing followers requires the leader to be able to refrain from using his height or her position as a means of power to encourage followers through the use of coercion or fear. One of the ways to prevent this concept of authority is through relinquishing control or command and truly seeking the opinion and wisdom of those in a level of lesser power within the organization.

Leadership power also comes from emotional power or model power. In such a situation, the leader is strong because of the role she or he represents or because of the emotional power associated with the role. An example of role power occurs with physicians or clergymen. Power in these circumstances allows the leader to influence or stimulate action among his or her followers. However, you must be especially careful in such a situation when discussing the views, beliefs, and concerns of someone who seeks your opinions regarding very critical and personal issues.

An example of someone with leadership power is Peyton Manning, the quarterback and MVP for the

Indianapolis Colts national football team. Manning is able to successfully motivate and move the offensive team down the field repeatedly to score points even when the weather is terrible and the team is behind in points.

The Powers of Persuasion

A leader is created and has power when other individuals align and act in concert with his or her cause. When a leader becomes a dictator or tyrant, followers will follow only because circumstances force them to obey—they are being pushed, not pulled.

A most effective method of moving people is the art of persuasion. Persuasion is a hard quality to define and an even more difficult skill to develop. Persuasion can be wonderfully effective to influence and move people, but to make persuasion work requires a lot of time and effort. And a poor or ineffective listener can foil successful persuasion. In essence, persuasion is the art of selling, defined for a specific purpose or cause.

In order to get people to follow you, and to align their thinking and acting with you, you must use persuasion tools. In his book the *Secrets of Power Persuasion*, Roger Dawson states that "the ability to persuade is the complex web upon which our whole world is suspended." In this book, Dawson identifies the foundation for power persuasion by looking at eight ways that influence people. According to Dawson, these keys are as follows:

- People can be persuaded if they think you can reward them.

- People can be persuaded if they think you can punish them.

- People will buy what you are saying if they think you can both reward and punish them.

- People can be persuaded if you have bonded with them.

- People can be persuaded if their options are limited in a specific situation.

- People can be persuaded if they think you have more expertise than they do.

- People can be persuaded if you act consistently.

Learning how to use these persuasion tools takes time and much practice. As noted above, persuasion is the art of selling. In order to effectively persuade, you must know your product, know the needs and wants of your audience, and create a memorable presentation to make the "sale." One significant factor is your level of enthusiasm. Your passion and conviction are powerful forces that will help move even the most stubborn resisters. You can use your enthusiasm and excitement to motivate and capture the attention of followers. Your enthusiasm can and will create enthusiasm and passion in others.

Personal Power Tools
Having power is an important asset. How do you get power and use it to your advantage? You must learn to use all resources and learn from the people around you who use power well. You can also learn by noticing how others respond to you and others in particular situations. Everyone around you is a good teacher if you watch and listen. People believe and do things for reasons based on their own opinions, knowledge, experience, and information. Individuals may not accept your rationale, but they may accommodate your stated reasons into their thinking (values and beliefs). You can also learn from mistakes that you make or observe among your colleagues, family members, or friends. Some of the best

methods for gaining power are built on your attitude and behaviors in positive and negative situations. Success Through Reinforcement of Attributes, the STAR Approach, relies on continued learning and growing. Use of the following attributes will help increase your power, your memorability, and your unforgettableness.

Possibility Thinking

As noted earlier, Reverend Robert Schuller enthusiastically describes possibility thinking. Possibility thinking is not false optimism, but a positive mental attitude. Possibility thinking is the willingness to believe in yourself and your abilities. Possibility thinking is a break from provincialism or the narrow way of thinking that keeps us from doing or trying something different. The possibility thinker can see new alternatives or options for old issues and is open to hearing new or different ideas and information. Possibility thinkers are able and willing to see how ideas, options, and concepts are constantly changing, offering new opportunities for improvement regularly. In other words, life and the world are ever changing with endless opportunities to move in new and different directions.

Possibility thinking can also be called lateral thinking. You may wish to consider the option of going sideways or diagonally for a result of improved outcome rather than only up or down. Vertical thinkers see only in black and white, yes and no, and either/or as options. Lateral thinkers see a rainbow of colors or options. Lateral thinkers think in terms of all possibilities within a range of solutions. As Schuller says, "If you see a possibility, seize it. Seize the possibilities in your life!"

Political Savvy

Politics often carries the connotation of scheming or dishonesty. However, if you want to be powerful and create a memorable impression, you must have some political savvy or knowledge in order to reach a leadership position. Many individuals are turned off by having to "play politics" at the office, but politics are part of the business game and the game of life. Both women and men must learn to develop relationships and a personal business style that is likeable or agreeable to others. Self-confidence and discernment of the key players and their agendas are crucial factors to understanding and participating in political savvy.

Being successful and memorable equates to more than just putting your head down and grinding out a good job or reasonably successful project. Equally important is your ability to work happily and well with others—to work well with both the individuals you like and with the individuals you dislike or find challenging, including those who are in positions of power or influence.

Again the concept arises that you have little ability to affect the changes that you believe are necessary for the greater good until you have proven yourself both capable and creditable. Political savvy takes time, perseverance, and oooooooooh so much patience and tolerance.

Prior Achievement
Nothing succeeds like success. In other words, success builds upon itself. To achieve a goal, your momentum comes from within. Achievement also can build up your creative anticipation and add to your reputation of success. Achievement increases the number of people who support and follow you, thus helping you to succeed. Effective leaders do not hide their accomplishments, but graciously let others announce this information. Or the leader may wish to present information in an advertising or promotional campaign.

The information is provided to others in a factual and non braggadocios manner. Achievement and knowledge of past successes will reinforce your position of credibility among followers and further strengthen your memorable image. A key point here is to *always* give credit to others. Remember you achieved your goal with the help of many other persons providing assistance. To gain followers, you need to credit all who have helped or assisted you along the way.

Poise

Poise is absolutely essential if you want to be an unforgettable and powerful person. Poise is the ability to be confident and keep your head up when the stuff hits the fan! Poise is described as an easy, self-possessed assurance of manner, a particular way of moving or carriage. In addition, poise is associated with behaviors and actions as you respond to and cope with people and situations. In order to develop poise and self-assurance, the process of self-evaluation, personal growth, and change must continue throughout your life. Poise is discussed further in Chapter Eight.

Pliability

Pliability is another word for flexibility—flexibility in your mind and in your life. Pliability is another essential component necessary to achieve power. To be effective, you must be able to change and adapt, to accept uncomfortable situations, and be able to find positions of compromise while maintaining your position, morals, and ethics—to have resiliency. A simplified definition suggests that, "Resiliency is the human capacity to face, overcome and even be strengthened by the adversities of life." Thus, to have resiliency in a difficult situation is to be able to implement or affect a positive adaptation within the context of significant or challenging adversity.

If you view compromise as a loss of position or status, you are giving up your power. The key to success is to keep your goal in mind and to do all that is needed to achieve that objective. If compromising helps you get what you want, you are not losing power provided you do not compromise the essence of who you are. When you compromise to achieve your goal, and someone benefits (to some degree) from that compromise, you are being pliable and maintaining your position as an effective and memorable leader,

Principles
To establish integrity, you must have firm values and principles upon which to base your opinions. In order to lead effectively and have leadership power, you must have established principles and values upon which you base your behaviors. As noted in Chapter Three, being memorable requires a commitment to a higher standard of principles. Being memorable carries with it a demand for goodness of character. All of us have influence and can affect the responses of others in our lives. When you achieve power, your ability to influence others may be remarkably easy at times. Yet even with power, having established values and principles will help you use your power more effectively and will reinforce the memorable image you wish to leave with others.

MANNERISMS THAT EMPHASIZE POWER

Some mannerisms clearly detract from and diminish our power and our goal of creating a memorable image. On the table below, mannerisms that diminish or enhance power and memorability are described.

Diminish Your Power	Increase Your Power
Plastering a smile on your face is unnatural and suggests falseness or trepidation.	Use appropriate facial expressions in conjunction with the conversation.
Constantly tilting your head when you talk or listen.	Keep your head level and use direct eye contact with speakers or listeners; don't appear to be indifferent or uninterested.
Perpetually nodding your head to encourage others to talk is reminiscent of the doggy in the rear window.	Let people know that you agree with them, but don't overdo it… you do not need to rescue the speaker.
Continually touching your body or stroking your moustache or beard, running your hands through your hair or tossing your head. Excessive or "nervous" movements, distractive hand gestures.	Relaxed and self-assured posture relays a sense of confidence and composure. Gestures should emphasize what you are saying through deliberate movements or gestures.

SUMMARY THOUGHTS FROM CHAPTER FIVE

Power is a prerequisite for accomplishment. To be unforgettable, you must learn to use power thoughtfully, judiciously, and effectively. Sharing power gives others the opportunity to reach conclusions, solve problems, and justify decisions. Goal power comes when a leader identifies a desired outcome and clearly articulates the outcome to followers. Communication power comes from being perceived as a credible source of ideas, actions, or messages on a topic or issue of importance. Follower power is based in part on the relationship between the leader and the follower(s). Leader power exists only if followership is achieved.

Tools to Use Power Successfully

- **Avoid an argument if at all possible**. Discuss differences, deliberate the issue, but don't argue. Keep the discussion impersonal and attack the issue, not the person.

- **Never tell a person she or he is wrong, even if it's true.** All this will do is deflate the other person's ego and escalate the situation. Remember, an effective leader works to fulfill the needs of followers. Rather than saying "you're wrong," suggest other options or a broader range of consideration.

- **If you are wrong, admit your mistake or error quickly.** You will not be blamed for being wrong as much as you will be admired for admitting your mistake.

- **Begin your discussion in a friendly tone.** If you begin the discussion in an angry or accusatory manner, you will quickly lose your audience. Smile warmly and give general information in your opening comments.

- **Initiate your position with a statement that supports agreement.** Open your discussion in a way that allows or encourages others to agree. If you can reach agreement initially, it is harder for others to disagree.

- **If disagreement occurs, let the other person talk about the project or situation.** Allow individuals to disagree. Often an individual will bring himself around and support your position through personal discussion and the opportunity to voice his or her opinions.

- **Give credit to others.** Remember that your goal is to change the thinking of your listeners. If the other person needs or wants to think she put forth the idea, who cares? As long as you accomplish your goal, authorship of ideas is trivial.

- **When appropriate, use empathy.** Honestly try to view a situation from the other person's point of view. Often you may learn something that will work to your advantage.

- **Whenever possible, add stimulating questions to the discussion.** By causing others to think, you may help convince them that your point is correct.

- **Dramatize your idea.** The use of short stories or examples will reinforce your point and can be persuasive.

- **Make an effort to fill a need.** Every human act is a response to the need of another. To persuade someone, you must show the benefits received through the actions taken.

- **Be wonderfully enthusiastic!** Enthusiasm that is based on the power of conviction is unbeatable. Enthusiasm is a powerful force that can sway even the most stubborn opponents. Strive for mutual gain through achieving a win-win position.

CHAPTER SIX

UNLOCKING YOUR POTENTIAL FOR CREATIVITY

To be perceived as a memorable person, you have to develop and polish your personality, attitude, and behavior, in ways that will distinguish you—in ways that will set you apart and make you worthy of being remembered well.

Creativity is a potent tool to increase success through the accomplishment of your goal to become a memorable person while achieving other goals in your life. Creativity is a personal expression often coming from an urge to improve or change the free flow of ideas in your mind. Creativity can act as an outlet for ideas that do not have a current application, provide an opportunity to work with others while developing new relationships, and give you the chance to express your innovative capabilities without the need for artistic talents.

Unlocking your potential for creativity involves a continuing process of building and enhancing your image. To some, this concept may sound like an expensive process, but this process doesn't require large outlays of cash, a famous birthright, social prominence, or a distinguished position. What you need most is high-image creativity. The skills developed through creative thinking really become useful in the continuing process of building and enhancing your image. Once you acquire a stirring or notable presence, your memorability is a shoo-in!

In fact, much of what goes into creating an unforgettable image involves the art and practice of creative thinking. Learning to develop this attribute will not only help you in your quest, but actually the attribute or skill, in and of itself, will make you more even memorable.

In an article titled "*About Creativity*," authors Bowd, McDougall, and Yewchuk developed some creative thinking abilities to help better understand creativity. The following are the creative thinking abilities they describe:

- *Fluency:* the ability to produce many responses to an open-ended question or problem
- *Flexibility:* the ability to generate ideas that are unconventional or to view a situation from a different perspective
- *Originality:* the ability to produce unique, unusual, or novel responses relative to one's reference group
- *Elaboration:* the ability to add rich and elaborate detail to an idea while developing and implementing it
- *Visualization:* the ability to imagine and mentally manipulate images and ideas to see them from different internal and external perspectives
- *Transformation:* the ability to change one thing or idea into another, to see new meanings, applications, and implications of something already in place
- *Intuition:* the ability to see relationships or make connections based on partial information
- *Synthesis:* the ability to combine parts into a coherent whole

Most of us have the capacity to be imaginative and to achieve creative accomplishments. In the past, we used to classify as creative only accomplishments that could be achieved by certain individuals, specifically artists, writers, composers of music, or scientists discovering a new gene or medical breakthrough. We deemed someone creative if she or he had the ability to discover or somehow express a totally new idea, concept, or thought.

Often, because of past experiences, you may believe you are not creative. If you do not know how to paint a dramatic landscape or portrait or write a compelling story, you may see yourself as lacking in creative abilities. Open your mind to the concept that all of us have creative persons, but for each of us, the creativity we express is different. How exciting—we are creative people!

From a broad perspective, creativity means perceiving things differently, interposing pieces in a new way to develop a different combination or arrangement in the big picture. Creativity involves innovation and inventiveness, and is often perceived as a gift rather than a skill. Either/or, it is a gift that we all have, though many of us have not fully learned how to use this gift to the best of our abilities.

The key to unlock your creativity is learning how to develop and strengthen your creative thought processes in ways that will support you professionally and help you become a more memorable and unforgettable person.

In the book *Creative People at Work*, authors Gruber and Wallace write that creative work takes a long time to occur. They state, "It (creative work) is not a matter of milliseconds, minutes or even hours—but of months, years and decades." Learning to perceive things differently, to be open and curious is a skill that can be developed at any age, and that can give interest or pleasure. Your experiences define your ability to perceive differently. Accepting this truth will allow you to develop this skill now and use it more effectively.

Developing creativity as a memorable attribute is a most rewarding experience. And although development of a new attribute does take time, creative thinking can be accomplished while you drive to work or ride the bus; while you wait in line, or enjoy a solitary walk. It works, and it's fun!

Creative Thinking

Embellishing creative talents requires creative thinking. Creative thinking requires an approach that for many of us is new. In order to think creatively, you must throw out old rules or limitations and open your mind to any and all possibilities. This approach may seem silly or a waste of time. But if you achieve the successful results you seek and a positive outcome, who cares? To indulge in creative thinking, you need to create a climate in which to work that encourages and supports your work and efforts. A creative climate must provide the motivation to encourage and challenge you to explore new ideas, thoughts, and positions.

Environments can be either supportive or obstructive and can both stimulate or distract your creative thought processes. You may have heard of the idea to "get up and take a walk" as a way to stimulate new thoughts and ideas. Changes in your surroundings will stimulate your brain, helping you to create new thoughts and enhancing your ability to generate new ideas. To establish or create a more inviting and effective creative workspace, you may wish to make changes in your office or a room in your home. Consider the following examples:

- Find music or other sounds that increase your ability to daydream or meditate.

- Add a piece of art, a plant, or some aromatic candles or oils.

- Find a pleasing texture to cover a favorite chair, cabinet or wall divider.

- Place a colorful rug on the floor or hallway.

- Rearrange the furniture or accessories in your office or favorite room at home.

By changing the space around you in a way that gives comfort and inspiration, in a way that makes you feel good, you will open your mind and begin to do all kinds of new and wonderful creative things.

Dr. Curt Bonk, in the School of Education at Indiana University, has identified several traits and thinking characteristics that he believes indicate creativity. The creativity traits identified by Dr. Bonk are related to products, attitudes, and behaviors and are shown below.

Creativity Traits
- *Products:* fluency, flexibility, originality, and elaboration.
- *Attitudes:* curiosity, imagination, complexity, risk-taking.
- *Behaviors:* flexible, imaginative, nonconforming, novel answers.

Thinking Characteristics
- Metaphoric thinking (new synthesis, perspective, transformation)
- Flexibility and skill in decision making
- Independence in judgment (not compelled by latest trends)
- Coping well with novelty (What if? and work with ideas)
- Logical thinking skills (evidence, conclusions, if-then, break set, unpredictable)

- Visualization (imagery, personal analogies)
- Escaping entrenchment (new angle/pattern, break set, unpredictable)
- Finding order in chaos (complexity in thought, asymmetrical images)
- Problem finding
- Evaluation

Through his work, Dr. Bonk has also identified traits and thinking behaviors that limit our abilities and efforts to change or take memorable actions and that may cause difficulty with participating in classes or organizations. He has identified the following potentially destructive traits:

- Tends to question laws, rules, authority
- Indifferent to common conventions and courtesies
- Stubborn, uncooperative, resists domination
- Argues the rest are out of step
- May not participate in class
- Argumentative, cynical, sarcastic, rebellious
- Demanding, assertive, autocratic
- Low interest in details
- Sloppy, careless, disorganized with unimportant matters
- Self-centered, intolerant, tactless
- Capricious
- Temperamental, moody
- Emotional, withdrawn, aloof, uncommunicative
- Forgetful, absent minded, mind wanders, watches windows
- Overactive physically or mentally

Dr. Edward de Bono, the originator of the term "lateral thinking," writes against the activity defined as crazitivity. This activity is described as creativity that is solely driven by the desire to be different. In a short article about crazitivity, Dr. de Bono states he has no objection to this style of creativity, but he fears that people will equate crazitivity with creativity. Crazitivity is the easy way to be noticed and to flaunt creativity, but as he writes, "creative contributions should deliver more value than just being different."

Intuitive Skills
Intuition is described as the ability to form insights and expectations without full knowledge or all of the information needed to analyze a situation or experience. Intuition is accumulated knowledge that is hidden away in the unconscious portion of our brains that surfaces as a "gut feeling." Intuition is what Napoleon Hill described in his book *Think and Grow Rich* as the "sixth sense." Often, though, you may ignore these feelings out of fear or uncertainty because you lack any basis of fact. As Michael Jordan says, "Limits like fears are often an illusion." Ignoring your intuition can and will limit your decision-making skills.

Developing your intuition is another way to increase your creative skills. To further develop your intuitive skills, you need to pay attention to what your body tells you. What is your gut reaction or response? Learn how to "read" your feelings, i.e., those gut reactions. Do you feel at ease, or do you feel threatened or uneasy? It does not matter why you feel uneasy or uncomfortable; the why is not relevant. Just take the time to assess the situation, and go with the feeling that best describes your internal perception. Another element mentioned often in the literature about intuition is not to work hard at being intuitive. Intuition is part of your subconscious mind and cannot be pulled in like something in your memory or relied upon to replace preparation (the old "wing-it" concept).

You can begin by testing or strengthening your intuition. A first step is to begin by guessing about everyday situations. For example, guess the number of voicemail messages on your telephone, estimate the number of gallons of gas your car will hold, how many people will get on the elevator at the next floor, or guess who is calling when the telephone rings. Learning to use your intuitive skills will greatly enhance your creative abilities. The following are some of the most commonly offered techniques to build or strengthen intuitive skills:

- Learn to sit quietly, to calm yourself, and relax while heightening your awareness of surroundings.
- Use word association games or problem-solving exercises.
- Learn to listen "actively." Minimize distractions, maintain eye contact, and really hear what is being said.
- Improve your visualization skills and imagination techniques.
- Open your mind to risk-taking—be an edge runner—have faith—Just Do It!

The key for staying creative is that you will need to live life differently and do things differently. One basic rule is to do something different each day. Here are a few other ideas to stimulate new thinking: eat out at a new place; drive a different route to work; begin a new exercise program; read a different kind of book; meet someone new, and hear their thoughts on current issues; pick a racier or more subdued tie; change your routine for applying makeup, or the process for changing the oil in your car, fixing dinner, organizing the papers on your desk, or arranging the tools in your garage.

You can learn to use your intuition to determine possible outcomes. Your attitude about the use of this tool must be open to all possibilities. A closed mind does not allow for change or new perceptions. Development of your intuition is a fundamental skill needed for good management, problem solving, and decision making. Learning to use your intuitive skills is not as difficult as you may think.

You can refine your intuitive skills by learning how to focus on an issue while paying close attention to the details of the situation, person, or place. Use of this mindful investigatory process will help you strengthen your capabilities for formulating effective insights, expectations or a course of action. Even without having all of the facts, the accumulated knowledge that is buried deep in your brain will be put to work to increase your perceptivity or "sixth sense."

Learning to use your intuition will help you assess ideas and thoughts in a more effective and rapid manner and will enhance your creative thinking skills and make you more unforgettable.

Blocking Creativity
Creativity can be blocked in a number of ways. Creative blocks can be associated with the idea mentioned earlier where based on past experiences you decide that you are not a creative person. You then let this thought process block attempts at creative development.

Generally, we have been trained to think and behave in conventional ways. Yet creativity requires a change of pace—a breaking of the rules. For many of us, powerful psychological blocks have been reinforced to help us maintain socially acceptable behaviors. While this process is very helpful most of the time, it does distract and damage individual creativity. To some extent, nonconformity should be valued and encouraged, teaching you to think divergently, emphasizing intellectual curiosity and freedom of exploration. As mentioned earlier, when taken to extreme, nonconformity can become disruptive.

Creativity is at times blocked by the people around you. If you seek approval of another person, you may not feel okay or comfortable presenting new or different thoughts and ideas for fear of disapproval from this person. Or the other person may provide negative comments about your work, your ideas, and your creative attempts in such a way as to discourage or dispel any notion of a creative process.

Creativity can be blocked by the silly notion that "It's just fluff!" For some people who work primarily with data or numbers, creativity may seem to be insubstantial or unscientific. Brainstorming or idea generating may be seen by some logical, structure-oriented people as a "total waste of time" or like "you're doing nothing, but sitting there saying things." Generating ideas, brainstorming, is the first real step in creative thinking—a vital and necessary requirement. Find individuals with whom you can exchange ideas and concepts, and cultivate an open-minded relationship with them. This process will help prevent inhibition of your creative selves from the more structured people and activities that are experienced in daily life.

Another way to stop or block creativity is to associate creative thinking with something you don't like or with which you are uncomfortable. For example, some people believe that persons who are artistic are more creative than those who are not. If you associate creativity with being artistic and you are not comfortable with the concept of being artistic, you may discount or find fault with a creative idea or plan simply because of your inept thinking.

You can also block creativity by thinking that it is difficult or hard to do. Coupled with that concept, you think you are not smart enough or do not have the clever mind that is needed to be creative. Remember, we are all creative, but we are creative in different ways and on different days. Creativity involves risk and uncertainty, doing something new or untried. There are many ways to kill creativity or creative thinking: laugh at it, analyze it, criticize it, ignore it, compete with it, change it, attack the messenger, or pass it off to a conflicted committee.

To think and support creative thinking is a challenge for each of us every day when we set out to be a memorable, unforgettable star. So here is my solution: clench your hands, shut your eyes, and *jump*!!!

Deliberate Creativity

Creativity is generally about "breaking the rules," seeing beyond limitations or long-held perceptions to put together new and different connections—that nonconformity thing. The phrase "thinking outside of the box" has become quite routine in our everyday pursuit of innovative ideas or problem-solving techniques. Yet often, as you set out to create something new and exciting, you run into a mental or organizational block. Your ideas are flowing and great, but then you cannot figure out how to go on or which direction to take to finish the project.

Many years ago, Alex Osborn and Sid Parnes developed the "Osborn-Parnes Creative Problem Solving Process." In 1948, Osborn published the book *Your Creative Process* and described the technique of brainstorming—using the brain to storm a problem and come up with a solution. This technique enables you to develop and practice the concept of deliberate creativity or the practice of thinking up of solutions based on unique new ideas. Learning the ability to brainstorm will help you learn the skills of deliberate creativity, and this skill will surely help you create an unforgettable image.

 Because it is often so hard to think out of the box, maybe you should forget that plan. Here's an idea I've learned from others, and it works. I've learned that moving to a new place physically often opens my mind to new ideas and thinking. In the literature, this is called "displacement."

The displacement concept focuses on physically going outside your usual surroundings to a new place. This change of scenery will allow your mind to open to new thoughts and ideas, and your brain will be inspired in new ways. Sometimes, just going for a walk around the block will help stimulate a stream of new ideas. Or stop what you are doing and exercise for ten to thirty minutes. Exercise increases the amount of glucose in the brain, and that activity increases brain activity and function. Glucose increases oxygen in the bloodstream that stimulates the brain to release endorphins and increase new connections. Exercising your body causes exercise in your brain! Going to a different place and being in new surroundings will definitely stimulate your mind, helping you generate new thoughts and ideas.

Another reason for further development of your creative skills is that medical research shows that creativity delivers growth to the brain. New studies in research show that our brains do not age like our bodies. Significantly, your attitude has much to do with the determination of how you age. A recent study in the Epidemiology and Public

Health Departments at Yale University found that older people with more positive self-perceptions of aging lived 7.5 years longer than did those with less positive perceptions.

Dr. Gene Cohen, a gerontologist and psychiatrist, says, "Everyone, of any age, must cultivate a creative and productive life." Cohen states that taking care of and developing relationships, sports, hobbies, religion, and volunteerism are as important to aging well as are diet and exercise. He believes that the last life stage, age after fifty, is the "liberation stage." And history reinforces his point with many people from Michelangelo to Mark Twain who became remarkably creative as they aged. Participation in leisure activities, such as book reading, board games, and playing musical instruments will help you maintain a more exciting and creative approach to life. Make an attempt to share your creative self with others and continue to grow.

SUMMARY THOUGHTS FROM CHAPTER SIX

Tools to Think Creatively

1) Believe your goal can be accomplished.
When you believe something can be achieved, your mind will find ways to bring about success. Begin by eliminating negative words and phrases from your mind. Don't think or say words like: impossible, won't work, can't do, there's no use trying, it's just too hard, or we've always done it this way.

2) Don't let tradition paralyze your mind.
Be receptive to new ideas and open to experiments. Try a new approach to an old problem, or try an old approach in a new way. Don't be a laggard, waiting until everyone else is using a new system or trend before you even begin to get comfortable with the old one.

3) Ask yourself daily, "How can I do better?"
Remember, there is no limit to self-improvement. All of us can do more or perform better, every day, in all that we do, for the rest of our lives.

4) Ask yourself, "How can I do more?"
Capacity is a state of mind. By asking yourself this question, you will put your mind to work to find solutions. In order to accomplish more, consider improving the quality of your work product or output and increasing the quantity of the work performed.

5) Learn to listen well.
Practice asking a question and then really listening, really hearing the response that the other person gives. Don't

try to form your response while listening. Just listen, think through what you have heard, and then respond.

6) Stretch your mind.
Associate with people who can and will help you think of new ideas or new ways of doing things. And when you hear these new ideas, remember points 2 and 5 above: really hear the information and be open to investigating or trying something new.

7) Take risks and see what happens.
Don't let the fear of failure or disapproval stifle your creativity. Open your mind, and stop thinking or straining to come up with a new idea. Just let your mind flow from one thing to another. Have fun and realize that sometimes creative brilliance is the outcome of spontaneous accidents.

CHAPTER SEVEN

UNLOCKING YOUR POTENTIAL FOR GOOD HEALTH

Memorable Health

Another aspect of creating an unforgettable image is the status of your health. Part of being memorable is maximizing your health status through disease prevention and appropriate disease management. If I asked you to give the name of someone that you remembered for health-related topics or histories, you might come up with quite a list. That is because the people you remember are memorable. They have said or done something that conjures up memories of health in either a positive or negative light. Positive examples include Lance Armstrong, Katie Couric, former Arkansas Governor Mike Huckabee, and Elizabeth Edwards. All have done or said something that has affected thousands of individuals. Their decisions and experiences influence the way that we think of a particular disease process or the decisions that we make to improve our own health. Sharing their courage and determination to maintain an active healthy life provides an example for each of us to follow.

Each of us has a responsibility to do what we can to maximize our health. Although we may have a predisposition to certain diseases or medical problems secondary to genetics or other causes, it is important to do what we can to prevent disease development or progression. You can maximize your health through a good mindset coupled with optimal choices, thereby providing the opportunity to achieve and reach goals and events that are important to you and others who care about you.

Because some of us may be confronted with what seems like overwhelming medical issues, it is important to understand that setting unrealistic goals can cause feelings of frustration, anger, or justified in giving up the whole process. A good balance is a fundamental key to success. As my good friend Kris says, "Life is, after all, for living."

An Appropriate Mindset

The most important aspect of developing a good health plan is starting with the appropriate mindset. To better understand how this works, I want to share the story of a determined young woman who worked in a medical practice. While in her early twenties, this young woman went on a tropical vacation with her siblings and parents. While participating in a sea kayak tour on one of the beach areas, her kayak overturned. Due to poor physical conditioning, she found it nearly impossible to get back into the kayak when in deeper water. This embarrassing moment caused her to make drastic changes in her lifestyle when she returned home.

Since she had struggled with being overweight from childhood, she decided that losing weight was *not* her goal. Repeated efforts in her life to achieve a weight that society considered appropriate had either resulted in a failure to lose weight, or after losing weight, she regained it. This young woman simply wanted to be strong and healthy enough to pull herself back into a boat if she fell out.

With this goal in mind, she met with an exercise specialist who worked with patients after heart attacks or strokes. Her plan was to exercise every day and eat foods that would make her stronger and healthier. She also made a deal with herself not to "deprive" herself of foods that she enjoyed, but decided to be mindful of what she really found good to eat.

The first day on the stair-master she went five minutes and had to stop. She felt terrible. She couldn't breathe and was severely fatigued. Several months later, this marvelous young woman zoomed along on the stair-master for a full hour. Sweat drenched her shirt while she worked to achieve her goal. She had achieved her desire to improve her strength and health. A side effect of her exercise was an eighty-nine pound weight reduction.

It is important to understand the steps to this young woman's success. Her goal was to become stronger and healthier so that she could participate in outings and events that she enjoyed. To achieve this goal, her plan was to exercise and eat differently.

Events or Activities for Good Health

What events or activities are important for you to participate in over the next twelve months to twenty-five years? For example, do you have family events, travel destinations, or business or community activities planned for the future? It is important not to fall into the classic trap of thinking of the event or activity as the change. Many of you will say that you want to look good or achieve a certain size before you attend an important event. In reality, the focus should be on the event and what you want to do while you are there. You may want to dance, stoop to pick up a child, or run alongside the newlywed's car as the bride and groom drive off.

List below the five most important events or activities in which you plan to participate. You should update this list at least four times every year.

_____

_____

_____

_____

_____

_____

Now, list the five activities in which you participate that contribute positively to your health and support the activities in the events noted above.

_____

_____

_____

_____

_____

What things do you want to change to improve your health status? For example, are you currently involved in regular exercise activities? Is your level of activity helping you create the unforgettable impression you wish to achieve? Or is your level of activity compromising your abilities to create a memorable impression and accomplish your health status goals?

List below changes you wish to make in your exercise program to improve health status:

_____

_____

_____

Disease Prevention

Disease prevention is best achieved through regular exercise, good dietary habits, and paying close attention to your body while undergoing age-appropriate health assessments. Many individuals sense when there is something physically wrong. Sometimes they are acutely aware of changes in their bodies or at other times they note a nonspecific change in the way they feel. Knowing your body well through regular self-examination is very important.

Women are much more likely through regular self-breast exams to catch an early malignancy. Men who perform regular testicular exams are more likely to find an early testicular cancer. In addition to listening carefully to your body, it is important to access age-appropriate diagnostic evaluations. Accessing diagnostic evaluations are much like maintaining a vehicle or home. It is usually much more cost-effective to follow the recommendations from the manufacturer for maintenance than it is to pay for the damage that occurs secondary to undiagnosed problems. Fortunately a vehicle or home can typically be salvaged after poor maintenance. Our bodies are not always as resilient.

Disease Prevention Assessments

Listed below are some recommended disease prevention assessments that you might request from your healthcare provider. Availability of scientific articles via the Internet has made it much easier for individuals to learn about and remain updated on the rapid changes in medicine. You are encouraged to become more involved in your health by accessing websites such as

WebMD, ClevelandClinic.org, Health.Harvard.edu, or the MayoClinic.com. Google offers the ability to access the same articles on the Internet that providers and healthcare agencies use to set guidelines and make recommendations.

Many times the information in these articles can take three to twelve months or longer to go from important information to a published guideline or recommendation. Thus, reviewing articles on the websites noted above may be the best source or method for attaining new information. That being said, it is important to recognize that some of these articles may have bias or other statistical concerns that make the information difficult to interpret. Although you are encouraged to seek out the latest information, be certain to read with scrutiny and temperance. Many reference groups are included in the information below so that you can access the information either online or by direct contact.

General information about several common health conditions follows. In no way is this information provided to serve as medical advice or recommendation. This information is provided as reference material. If you have questions, first and foremost, talk with your personal healthcare provider.

Diabetes (High Blood Sugar): Undergo annual glucose (sugar) testing with more frequent evaluation if you develop symptoms such as excessive thirst, frequent urination, visual changes, or unexplained weight loss or if you already have diabetes or hyperglycemia. If you have diabetes, it is very important to follow the recommendations set forth by the ADA, American Endocrinology Association, or other reliable guidance groups such as the New Mexico Takes on Diabetes (NMTOD), which has a most helpful website.

Hypertension (High Blood Pressure): Have your blood pressure checked at least annually and monthly or quarterly if your blood pressure is elevated. Checking an elevated blood pressure several times a day can cause it to raise secondary to apprehension and anxiety. Hypertension is a silent killer as individuals rarely have any symptoms. Longstanding uncontrolled hypertension frequently results in heart attack, strokes, kidney disease, blindness, and peripheral vascular disease, so early intervention is critical. The American Heart Association is an excellent resource for information regarding diseases associated with hypertension.

Hypercholesterolemia: Have your cholesterol checked at least annually if it has been abnormal or if you have a family history of heart disease or stroke. If you have high blood pressure, pre-diabetes, or diabetes, it may be necessary to have your cholesterol checked much more frequently. If your cholesterol is normal, rechecks every few years may be appropriate if the values remain normal. Remember that a total cholesterol value under 200 means little without knowing HDL, LDL, and triglyceride levels. Medical practitioners know that a low HDL (High Density Lipoprotein) is as important in the development of vascular disease as is having a high LDL (Low Density Lipoprotein). There is also new evidence that there are some protective forms of LDL and some athrogenic forms of HDL. This new evidence makes it even more important to have a healthcare provider help you understand the risks associated with your cholesterol levels. Again the American Heart Association is an excellent resource for information regarding cholesterol and vascular disease.

Heart Disease: To help prevent heart disease, you need to have annual evaluations of blood pressure, diabetes, and cholesterol levels as described above. An annual EKG may be recommended if you are over age fifty or earlier if you have diabetes, hypercholesterolemia, or hypertension. If at any time you develop symptoms such as chest pain, become easily fatigued, have shortness of breath with activity, or feel neck or jaw pain with activity, you should seek medical attention immediately. It is important to understand that not everyone has chest pain when having a heart attack, especially if you have diabetes. Some may experience only profuse sweating, shortness of breath, severe onset of fatigue, neck (throat) pain, or indigestion and nausea or vomiting. Remember that early intervention not only saves lives, it can also improve long-term conditions.

General Women's Health: Having a PAP smear and mammogram are important parts of an annual routine examination. The frequency and necessity of these procedures varies depending upon age and risk factors such as family history, sexual history, and past medical and surgical history. If you find or feel a breast lump, but have had a normal mammogram, it is important to seek further evaluation with an examination by your healthcare provider. The American Cancer Society provides an excellent source of information regarding these important, potentially lifesaving tests.

General Men's Health: PSA or Prostate Specific Antigen is a screening test used to assess men for potential prostate cancer. This test is typically performed annually in men over age fifty unless the individual has a family history of prostate cancer when earlier evaluation may be warranted. Regular monthly self testicular exam is an important screening tool for testicular cancer. Remember that testicular cancer can occur in very young men, often in teens and early twenties, so start early and seek care quickly for any changes that occur. The American Cancer Society is an excellent resource for information regarding these tests.

Gastrointestinal Screening: It is recommended that individuals undergo colon cancer screening by age fifty. If an individual has symptoms or a family history of gastrointestinal cancers, a colonoscopy may be recommended at an earlier age. Although colonoscopy is an excellent test to diagnose the cancer, your healthcare provider may recommend a stool guiac test with or without a sigmoidoscopy. Once again, excellent information regarding these tests is provided by The American Cancer Society.

Bone Health: A bone density test is important to evaluate the potential risk for bone weakness that may lead to fractures. This test is typically recommended for postmenopausal women or men over age seventy and in individuals with increased risk for the development of osteoporosis. The National Osteoporosis Foundation is an excellent source for learning more about preventing, evaluating, and treating osteoporosis.

Immunizations: Everyone should receive a tetanus immunization every ten years unless there is an injury requiring an earlier booster. Discuss the importance of hepatitis A and/or B vaccine with your regular practitioner. Other vaccines may be necessary for travel outside the United States. Some vaccines require several months to complete the series, so seek a travel specialist's guidance several months prior to anticipated travel.

Complementary or Alternative Health Therapies: Although the above mentioned websites represent a traditional Western Medicine approach to health and wellness, many individuals seek complementary or alternative health therapies. You may wish to consider alternative or complementary disease prevention modalities alone or in combination with traditional practices and procedures of Western Medicine.

Acupuncture and massage therapy can be particularly helpful in overall wellness as well as acute and chronic musculoskeletal issues. Along with a good exercise and stretching program, these services can aid in substantially reducing chronic pain syndromes and stress reduction while helping to maintain overall health and wellness. Remember to seek a provider who is trained and certified in the modality of care in which you are interested.

Acupuncture is an ancient source of care that seeks to balance the forces with your body thereby leading to a healthier emotional/spiritual and physical self. A doctor of Oriental Medicine takes an extensive personal history and then may strategically place hair-like fine needles into the body at specifically defined points. These providers are also trained in the use of Chinese herbs and may recommend herbs in conjunction with acupuncture or other therapies.

Massage therapy is a process that seeks to balance the musculature and energy sources of the body via various massage methods. This treatment can be particularly helpful in overall wellness as well as in acute and chronic musculoskeletal issues. Along with a good exercise and stretching program, massage therapy can aid in substantially reducing chronic pain syndromes and stress while helping to maintain overall good health and wellness.

Some individuals find chiropractic medicine of great benefit for both acute and chronic medical issues. Learning about the various types of chiropractic training can be very helpful in selecting the best chiropractic specialists for you. Similar to practitioners of Oriental Medicine, chiropractors seek to balance the body in order to create a vessel of wellness, allowing the body to heal itself with support of appropriate musculoskeletal alignment. Some chiropractic providers also dispense homeopathic therapies for both acute and chronic medical issues. The Internet is an excellent resource to learn of various types of chiropractic training and can be helpful selecting the best alternative health provider for your needs.

Naturopathic Medicine is a similar to Western Medicine in many respects, but has a shorter, narrower training process and uses homeopathic therapies rather than standard pharmaceuticals. Herbologists are often trained in massage therapy or chiropractic medicine, but may also be traditional healers such as cundanderas or Medicine Men in a community. Spiritual Healers vary substantially in their beliefs and practices depending on the community where they work, such as the traditional medicine man, evangelical Christian healers, and mystics. Cultural Healers provide alternatives if you are seeking a more natural/spiritual approach to health and wellness. Ayurvedic Medicine is becoming a more commonly sought form of healthcare in the United States and includes some traditionally trained Western Medicine physicians who have added Ayurvedic training to their skills and knowledge base.

Behavioral Health

In order to maximize your health, it is vital to address your mental health and overall state of well being. Often you may find time to exercise your body, but forget to allot time for maintaining a healthy mind. This includes the reduction of stress in your life. Exercise is an excellent outlet for stress, and although an excellent modality for treating stress, adding some form of regular meditation or prayer may augment the benefits that you achieve from your health regime.

To help with acute or chronic issues, seeking help from a mental health professional may be imperative to moving forward toward your goals. You may have developed unhealthy ways of dealing with various life issues. You act through a collective of lifelong experiences that result in an action or verbal statement in response to a stimulus or lack thereof. Because of this, at times your responses may be more appropriate than at other times. If so, you may find that you have to deal with things in a way that creates inappropriate conflict, withdrawal, or a sense of regret. It is important to understand that is normal to make good decisions *most* of the time. However, that is to say that no one is perfect, and that is okay, too. Many excellent books are available to help develop healthier interpersonal relationship behaviors.

Although for the majority of the time, most of you will view yourself accurately, you may experience moments every day when others hear or believe that you have said something differently than you intended. This breakdown in communication can occur for many reasons including simple gender differences, but it may also be the result of an underlying mental health issue that has not been addressed.

For example, you may be unaware of your depression, anxiety, or anger, but express these feelings as irritability. Or you self-treat through unhealthy lifestyle choices such as apathy, drinking excessive amounts of alcohol, abusing drugs, purging, under or overeating, or exercising to extreme. Assessing the way you feel when you react inappropriately to various circumstances can help you recognize the need to seek help through your primary or mental healthcare provider.

Some of you may be working through complicated childhood issues, marital issues, gender issues, or financial concerns. All of these issues can create an incredible amount of stress. Although there may not seem to be easy answers to your problems, there are capable individuals trained to help find the best ways to cope with and resolve problems. Seek out the help you need, and don't allow negative life issues to keep you from accomplishing your life goals and the new image you seek.

Typically, at this point, you would be asked to list the issues or problems that may concern you or for which you may seek help. However, given the delicate nature of mental health, just make a mental note of the issues or briefly write your thoughts on a separate paper so that you can address them in privacy, rather than responding by listing the issues in this book.

Memorable Behaviors

At times, when interacting with others, you may be completely unaware of behaviors or expressions you use that leave negative unforgettable remembrances. Since each of us brings our life experience into everyday interactions, we display behaviors that we may have adopted since childhood. These behaviors are so much a part of who we are that we cannot see the negative effects that they may have on others. For example, you may find yourself easily becoming part of a volatile interaction by lashing back, rather than attempting to defuse a confrontive situation. You may find yourself whining with the rest of the pack, rather than attempting to find solutions.

Because of unresolved emotional issues, some of us may even find pleasure in creating, participating in, or watching turmoil and drama, rather than attempting to maintain a professional happy environment. This behavior will certainly cause you to be memorable. But do you want your headstone to read "Trouble Maker"? Probably not, especially if it could read "The one who brought out the best in others." If you feel like or think you may have negative behaviors, it is important to address this issue sooner rather than later. The longer you practice any particular behavior the harder it will be to overcome or remove it.

What specific patterns of behavior among your interactions may conflict with your desire to be positively memorable? List five things that you do that don't allow you to interact with others in a way that is rewarding?

_____

_____

_____

_____

_____

You may wish to seek help from a psychologist or other behavioral health specialist to find ways to improve or change your interactions. Making such changes can be difficult, but it is time and energy that is well spent and will likely result in a better, more satisfying life for you.

Who to See for Mental Health Questions

Psychologists and appropriately trained *social workers* provide an excellent resource for counseling and direction. These professionals can help individuals learn more about themselves, address unhappy or unhealthy relationships, and provide support in recognizing and potentially changing unhealthy behaviors. Generally, psychologists and licensed counselors are typically master and PhD level trained and are covered by most health insurance plans. Psychologists are also able to prescribe medications in some states. *Psychiatrists* are medical or osteopathic doctors who usually provide more medical care for chronic mental health issues such as bipolar disorder or schizophrenia and frequently provide more medication management than do psychologists. Psychiatrists are also trained to provide psychotherapy, but often work in conjunction with a psychologist or licensed therapist to provide counseling services.

Health Maximization

To achieve total health means maximizing health status by providing your physical, mental, and spiritual self with appropriate attention and care. Maximized health status is to become mindful of your health and well being and starts with awareness and action. To develop a plan of action, you must feel empowered. To begin this process, you should refuse to be called by the name of the disease, such as diabetic or asthmatic. It is interesting to see how healthcare providers have chosen to define some patients as being of the disease and others as having the disease. For example, someone with a history of malignancy is defined as a cancer survivor or as having cancer, but a person with diabetes is referred to as a diabetic. We speak of individuals as having depression and state that others are schizophrenic.

Definitions of having disease are quite different from being the disease. You are encouraged to shed these labels and to correct others, including the medical providers that you choose to work with who use this language. Labels inhibit management of the disease and displace your power in terms of participating in the activities that reduce the effects caused by the disease process. A person with diabetes manages the disease. Conversely, as the term *diabetic* implies, a person labeled as a diabetic is managed by the disease. The tail does not wag the dog. Empowerment results when you feel that the decisions you make result in outcomes associated with your choices.

Refusing to be labeled as a disease is an example of removing a negative attribute and replacing it with a positive attribute that changes the impression you feel and therefore create. By acknowledging that you are a wonderful individual who happens to have a disease process allows you to manage how the disease affects you and the perception you put forth. Another powerful step in disease management is learning to maintain your life activities while you have the disease. Allowing the disease to control your activities and behaviors is allowing the disease to control your life.

This is not to say that individuals who have disease processes that make them feel ill may not choose to participate in certain events or activities. The difference is the concept of choice and decision rather than allowing the disease process to victimize you. Most of us have been blessed to know individuals who shared their life experiences with cancer. Cancer tends to raise a sense of fear like few other illnesses, yet those who have experienced a cancer diagnosis are often the most well balanced individuals encountered. They seem to lose the need to control the disease, and learn instead to live with it. They *manage* the process and their lives rather than trying vainly to *control* it. Such should be the case with diabetes and other disease processes.

Another vital step in disease management is determining the stage you are in with respect to your disease process. Many years ago, Diane Kubler-Ross found that individuals go through several steps in order to reach a point of acceptance with respect to significant life changing events. These concepts were initially applied to death, but were found to be true of all major life events.

Kubler-Ross identified the following five steps:
    Denial
    Anger

Bargaining
Depression
Acceptance

These "stages" may not come in order, and some individuals may skip over or quickly through one or more of them. Becoming caught on one of these stages can prevent you from being able to move forward to manage life along with the disease process. For example, a person in denial of diabetes is unlikely to make the dietary changes necessary to improve blood sugar levels because she doesn't really believe she needs to do so. A person who is overweight may bargain, agreeing to participate in an exercise program as long as he sees adequate changes, but not committing to a permanent lifetime exercise program that will result in a healthier body habitus. Once you acknowledge your disease process, you can then make choices that will help you maintain and improve your total good health.

To maximize your health status, it is important to set short- and long-term life goals that support the unforgettable impression you wish to achieve. A short-term life goal may be to travel to another country on your vacation. A long-term life goal may be to remain independent and live in your home as you grow older. To achieve these goals, it is vital to maximize and maintain good health during all phases of your life.

Visualization for Disease Management
Another function that will help you to achieve your goal is visualization. You may visualize what you are thinking or you may plan what you will do for the day or what you will wear to an event. Visualization is an activity that you perform every day, often without thinking about what you are actually doing. What you visualize effects your attitudes, behaviors, and reactions to others and actions that occur.

Stop for a moment, close your eyes, and visualize or see yourself doing or completing one of the life goals you have identified on the first page of this chapter. Think about how you feel and how being able to achieve this life goal adds to your sense of overall well being.

Going one step further is the power of creative visualization. Creative visualization uses the powers of thought and imagination to help you create major life changes. Creative visualization is the technique of using your imagination to create those changes that you would like to occur in your life. Because of deep-seated negative concepts about life, you may have unconsciously expected and imagined lack, limitation, difficulties, and problems to be the outcome that occurs every day in your life. The opposite can also be true. Visualizing yourself participating in the new choices that you have decided to implement has been shown to be very helpful and effective. Some studies have shown that visualization actually improves physical endurance and encourages the body to be more physically active. Creating a positive unforgettable impression with a healthy lifestyle gives you the opportunity to be a role model for your family, friends, and community.

You can begin each day by visualizing what you have planned for the day and how you see these planned activities occurring. What sounds do you hear? What do you smell and see? What positive feelings do you associate with these choices, and how do they feel? Think about the goals you wish to accomplish or the tasks that need to be completed. Close your eyes and see yourself doing each goal or task; feel how you will feel when the goal or task is accomplished. In your mind, experience the success you feel when you accomplish your goals or tasks. As you accomplish your goals, see yourself as the positive memorable person you are.

List the things that you see, feel, smell, and hear. For example, if you have chosen to take up walking, picture yourself walking in a safe environment that is accessible to you. Can you feel the muscles in your legs getting stronger? Can you feel your heart and lungs developing an increased endurance? What is the temperature of your skin? Is the sky light, dark, or cloudy? Can you smell the scent of flowers, auto exhaust, or the hint of approaching rain? Do you hear music, the sound of traffic or a train, or maybe the melody of a bird calling from a treetop? What do your senses tell you, and how does what you see, smell, or hear make you feel in response?

Take the time to sit and write out your feelings and impressions. Use as much space as you need to re-experience your outdoor activity, and describe the senses you experience.

_____

_____

_____

_____

_____

_____

_____

_____

_____

_____

_____

_____

SUMMARY THOUGHTS FROM CHAPTER SEVEN

Maximizing Your Health

1. **Set life goals that are renewed at least quarterly.**

   Be responsible for maximizing your good health.

2. **Don't seek and expect a quick fix.**

   Work hard, and remember, you don't get something for nothing.

3. **Develop and maintain a regular dietary and exercise program.**

   Establish an appropriate mindset and positive attitude that supports your good health.

4. **Seek out friends who have similar interests in health and wellness.**

   Finding friends with similar interests makes dietary and exercise programs easier and more fun.

5. **Find a work environment that supports health and wellness.**

   Many companies encourage and support wellness programs. If a wellness program is not available, suggest options to your boss or the human relations department.

6. **Develop and maintain a long-term relationship with a healthcare provider.**

   A healthcare provider who knows you and your lifestyle will be more capable of responding appropriately to needs and issues in your life.

7. **Regularly review and implement your visualization for being memorable.**

    Use creative visualization to help initiate major life changes. It works—so try it!

8. **A good balance is key to success. Life is, after all, for living.**

CHAPTER EIGHT

UNLOCKING YOUR POTENTIAL FOR POISE

Poise, the polishing stone of personal presence, adds an element of graciousness and class. Similar to the power component, memorable people are almost always poised. But simply having poise does not necessarily make one an unforgettable person. Prestige, your standing or position in the eyes of others, is another key factor vital to becoming a memorable person. In order to have a commanding or strong personal presence, one must be perceived as poised and influential. Knowing how to successfully develop and use personal presence leads to this perception.

Poise is described as an easy, self-possessed assurance of manner, a particular way of moving or carriage. In addition, poise is associated with behaviors and actions as you respond to and cope with people and situations. In order to develop poise and self-assurance, the process of self-evaluation, personal growth, and change must continue. The word *poise* and what it means helps identify the images you seek and practice in order to become a memorable person.

To help clarify your definition of poise and as a reference, the following diagram indicates adjectives associated with the word *poise*.

POISE DIAGRAM

P	O	I	S	E
Positive	Open	Intuitive	Stable	Effective
Persuasive	Optimistic	Interested	Sensitive	Equilibrium

Developing a poised presence adds the finishing touches to your memorable image. As noted in Chapter Five, poise is absolutely essential if you want to be in a powerful position.

A professional colleague tells a story when he worked as s sales person for a large healthcare vendor. While at dinner in the hotel one night, this single and handsome fellow sent a drink to the table of a pretty woman dining alone. She smiled and continued reading her book and eating her salad. Somewhat encouraged, Jack asked the waitress to take another glass of wine to the woman. He smiled at the woman and gave a friendly wave of his hand. The woman quickly paid her bill and left the restaurant. The next morning at the community hospital, Jack bumped into the hospital president who was touring the facility with a consultant, who.....Yikes! happened to be the woman in the hotel restaurant. Jack remained cool and calm during introductions, but later described how embarrassed and rattled he felt during the episode.

Poise is the ability to be confident and keep your head up when the stuff hits the fan! Poise gives you the skill to roll with the punches, to work under pressure, persist with a difficult job, and be decisive in the face of adversity. If you can "keep your cool," your coworkers and colleagues are also likely to remain coolheaded. What we have all seen or experienced are the escalating effects of a crisis—deadline dates, irate customers, or a jammed copy machine during a board meeting. Nothing is more stressful than to "lose it" while struggling to fix whatever is causing the instant crisis in our lives.

So, the questions are: How do you manage stress with poise and self-confidence? How do you overcome adversity and difficulties while maintaining a calm, cool presence? How do you keep that charming, memorable image intact? How do you create an unforgettable presence?

One key answer seems to be "don't panic!" You need to stay calm, remain focused, identify issues, be positive, and act confidently as you handle the crisis and accompanying stress. You must believe in your capabilities and your ability to manage the situation—to control or influence what we can and let the rest go. Like the Serenity Prayer states, "God grant me the serenity to accept the things I cannot change; the courage to change the things I can; and the wisdom to know the difference." If we could all adopt or incorporate this prayer into our daily lives, it would be soooooooooooooo much easier.

Peace of Mind

In his book *Maximum Achievement*, Brian Tracy says that the lack of peace of mind is the starting point for stress and negativity. To achieve peace of mind, he says three steps are needed:

1) Accept 100 percent responsibility for your decisions.

2) Prioritize your activities.

3) Concentrate your efforts on one activity at a time.

Tracy believes that by making peace of mind your highest goal, you will secure happiness and success. A certain element of poise comes from having peace of mind. Peace of mind or internal peace is a condition of being emotionally and mentally at peace with yourself and the issues around you. When you feel this sense of calmness and tranquility, a certain element of poise settles around you and allows you to focus more clearly and to react with a coolheadedness. Inner peace helps you feel stable, grounded, and poised. Having poise reflects a positive mental attitude and confident image—a memorable and unforgettable image.

Marian Woodall says to "Be Poised and Be Proud!" In her book *Thinking on Your Feet*, Woodall states that thinking on your feet means buying time before you speak. She believes that communication poise comes from the ability to talk comfortably about whatever topic is being discussed. Woodall says never has the need been greater for learning the skills and using the power that comes from saying what needs to be said in such a way that the listener can hear and understand.

If you respond to an issue and sound unprepared, you will lower your poise and lessen confidence in yourself, leading to a loss of credibility. Woodall's main point: think briefly before you speak. If you are working on a project or program, develop some "talking points." Your colleagues and others will surely ask questions: How is the project going? Are there any big problems? When will the project be completed? Think through the questions and your possible answers to determine what you want to say. Writing out the answers and keeping them handy to review or update from time to time will help you be better prepared when the questions come.

Frequently, prior to a presentation, if you quickly rush through information and feel comfortable that you know it, you may stumble when questioned or asked to describe what you have read. This bauble is because you recognize the information, but do not have it committed to memory. My suggestion is to fully write out everything that you plan to talk about or think will be discussed. This process will help you become more familiar with the material and be reassured when you respond to questions or provide a description of what you have learned. Review your written materials as often as possible before the presentation until you feel comfortable with the knowledge base and your understanding.

Also recognize that what you may think is vital information may not be relevant to those hearing your presentation. Think about the people attending the presentation, and define the content and depth of discussion. Often when individuals with different social styles (discussed later in this chapter), different types of jobs (like accounting or marketing), or different genders hear information, some very different interpretations may occur. Simplify the information, making it as understandable as possible to people from various different backgrounds. Try to learn as much as you can about "reading" others. It will make life easier in the long run and more successful.

Social Styles

There are four social styles or personality types recognized in the literature and everyday life. In the book *Personal Styles and Effective Performance*, Merrill and Reid believe that we learn to cope with others through our social styles. Each of us uses all four styles, but each person functions most often with the one style with which she/he is the most comfortable.

A key for learning how to create a memorable image is understanding how assertiveness and responsiveness interact and how these interactions affect responses. Learning your social style and being able to identify the social style of the person (s) you are communicating with will help you effectively adapt to that person's style.

Your social style manifests your habitual behaviors and interactions with others. This social style demonstrates your level of comfort or assurance in a particular situation. Social style has nothing to do with the innermost workings of your personality. It is simply how you act and what you do or say in a specific situation. Do you ask questions, pause to hear a response or issue commands? Do you devote more time to profit and loss or to the people with whom you work? Do you calmly accept information or requests from others?

The importance of knowing these different social styles will help you maintain or enhance your position in an organization, in your community, and with family members. Learning how to identify different social styles among co-workers and colleagues will help you understand the behavior of others while achieving your goal of becoming a memorable extraordinary person. Frequently, you may respond to another person based on your own style without recognition of the other person's needs or style, and the result is often confrontation. This conflict can be avoided by first recognizing the needs and social style of the person with whom you are communicating. This key step will result in better communication and interactions leading to a more positive memorable moment.

There are four basic social styles, and most people adopt one style with which they are comfortable and use this style more frequently than the others. The four social styles are

Analytical   Driver

Amiable   Expressive

One social style does not work any better than another one. However, the ability to relate well and get along with co-workers and family members is a major factor with each social style. The key to all of this is figuring out your social style and then matching it to the people around you. Following is an outline of each social style and some of the main characteristics or behaviors associated with that style.

Expressive Social Style
A person with an expressive social style is outgoing, flamboyant, and erupting with creative flashes. She expresses her emotions often and easily. People with an

expressive social style appear warm and approachable, but they are often competitive in their personal relationships. They want to be the best!

An expressive social style is generally seen in a person with strong self-confidence. His ideas reflect imagination and brilliance. Someone with an expressive social style can often put together components of a puzzle quickly or with little obvious thought. This person often makes decisions based on intuition or a hunch, and frequently that intuitive skill is accurate. Often though, a person with an expressive social style may change direction suddenly and fail to explain the reasons for making these changes.

Common characteristics or traits of someone with an expressive social style: enthusiastic, exciting, sociable; good at motivating others; reacts quickly and often intuitively; spontaneous, outgoing, and friendly with some need to be accepted; tends to use opinions and stories versus facts and data; easily able to visualize and idea oriented; animated and often shows feelings through facial expressions; speaks quickly and directly and has good direct eye contact.

People with an expressive social style may be perceived as dramatic, excitable, undisciplined, impulsive, and overly reactive. Under stress, an individual with an expressive social style may resort to personal attack.

Analytical Social Style

People with an analytical social style contain or control their emotions and rarely express feelings or acknowledge their feelings to others. They come to conclusions slowly and with what appears to be painstaking difficulty. This social style requires facts and lots of them. A person with an analytical social style wants as much information or data as he can possibly get, and he will ask many questions before diligently studying the data received.

An analytical social style tends to foster behavior traits that others may see as a nitpicker or as my son Eric defines as a "buzz killer." The analytical personality may seem more interested in getting one point right rather than in meeting the deadlines established for submitting a report. A person with an analytical social style will also be cautious about extending friendship and showing personal warmth. He may appear cool or distant when meeting with others and often will not participate in outside business activities unless required to do so.

Common characteristics or traits of a person with an analytical social style: orderly, precise, methodical and follows the rules; needs to be right; task oriented using facts and data; speaks slowly and has a slow reaction time; tends to avoid eye contact and controls facial expressions.

People with an analytical social style may be perceived as industrious, organized, indecisive, critical, exacting to the point, serious, and dull. When stressed, individuals with an analytical social style avoid conflict.

Driver Social Style
People with a driver social style appear to know what they want, where they are going, and how to get there quickly. Their motto is "Let's get the job done now, and let's do it my way!" Individuals with this social style are often loud, confrontational, and strongly certain that their way is the best and only way to accomplish a task.

For some people, working with a person who has a driver social style can be most difficult and challenging. A person with a driver social style may be confronting and demanding. The behaviors and demands of someone with a driver social style may intimidate people who must work with him or her. Because of a fear of being chewed up, people do not want to give bad news or contrasting opinions that do not match the ideas of the driver person. Drivers push for concrete results rather than for pleasing the people with whom they work. People with a driver social style do not seem to be caring people and often seem to be cold, indifferent, and autocratic.

Common characteristics or traits of a person with an driver social style: action-oriented with a need to see results, now and fast; speaks and acts quickly; short and fast reaction time; makes direct eye contact often with a rigid body posture and controlled facial expressions; uses data and factual information, but eliminates time on pleasantries.

People with a driver social style are often perceived as dominating and results oriented with little concern for others. They are comfortable with power and control. When under stress, driver personalities become very autocratic.

Amiable Social Style
Individuals with an amiable social style place a high priority on friendships and close relationships. They very much want and need cooperative behaviors from others around them in their work situation and in their personal lives. A person with an amiable social style is almost always perceived by others as a "really nice" person and may be remembered well for that trait.

When building a team in the workplace, people with an amiable social style make excellent team members. They are cooperative and easy to work with. However, while team members with an amiable social style may get along well with others, they have great difficulty making decisions. In fact, people with an amiable social style frequently will not give an opinion or may not even have an opinion on a particular issue. They often just agree to get along. For an individual with an amiable social style, getting along with others is the most important aspect of any outcome. So he will side with or agree with whoever is speaking because he does not want to hurt the feelings of a co-worker or friend.

Common characteristics or traits of a person with an amiable social style: acceptance and security; avoids conflict and will agree with others to do so; wants to be liked and to help others; friendly and agreeable; has an animated facial expression, but avoids direct eye contact; speaks slowly using opinions rather than facts and data.

People with an amiable social style are often perceived as uncertain, pliable, dependent, conforming, or weak. When stressed, individuals with an amiable social style will comply with others to avoid conflict and maintain relationships.

In summary, if new ideas or concepts are needed, people with an amiable social style are not the best choices unless you want to pass along new information to this group. Creativity or a wild run of imagination is highly unlikely to occur when working with someone with an amiable social style or an analytical social style. If there is a need for objective opinions and frank discussions, people with an expressive or driver social style may be of greater value even though they are more difficult with whom to work. People with an amiable social type can be excellent in customer service and quality improvement endeavors.

If quick decisions and direct-to-the-bone opinions are needed, people with an expressive or driver social style are the best choices. Agreement between members of these two social styles may be difficult because of other characteristics that make confrontation highly possible between these two different styles. When factoring this information into your life, please understand that many of us regularly display and interact using all of the styles depending on the behaviors and interactions of others and their role participation in a project or event. Some individuals often mirror or complement your social style(s) or that of another group member and thus become easy to recognize. Do not mistake this person as someone with an amiable social style. Often, they are "playing the game" and are capable of being quite competitive with others.

Clues to Social Style

There are some obvious clues to determining the social styles of the people with whom you work or play. Listed below are some of the more obvious clues to deciphering social styles.

1) The pace at which the person operates.

- How fast does he make decisions or get things done?

- How competitive is the person, not in sports, but in conversations with others?

- Does he joust for "airtime" in a meeting?

- How hard does he compete for the chance or opportunity to make a decision?

- How often does he suggest or tell others what needs to be done?

2) Look at the feelings emanating from the person when she communicates.

- How often does she smile?

- Is direct eye contact made with all attendees in the room?

- How broadly does she gesture or make expansive motions with her hands?

- Listen for emotional content in her comments—"I feel" versus "I think" comments.

The social style of a person is measured in relationship to three behavioral components. These components are:

- Assertiveness

- Responsiveness

- Versatility

Many articles in the literature describe how these scales measure social style, and I've interpreted this information for clarity. The assertiveness scale focuses on "tell behavior," and measures the degree to which a person tries to influence the decisions or actions of another by "tell behavior" or by asking questions ("ask behavior"). Tell behavior is risk taking, fast paced, and challenging while "ask behavior" is cooperative with deliberate actions and minimal risks. People who are assertive are confident and happy to argue their point or make their case while someone who is less assertive may be passive in his or her approach.

Responsiveness is measured by the degree that a person openly expresses feelings or controls feelings—a willingness to respond to others with the parameters being control and emote. Emotive behavior is oriented to relationships and is open and warm with the person often giving lots of information. Controlled behavior is serious, more disciplined, and cool with an unwillingness or inability to respond to others.

Versatility relates to your ability to adapt quickly and easily to the needs of another person. In today's rapidly evolving world, the ability to change or fluctuate readily is a most desired trait or behavior that allows you to improve and enhance interpersonal relationships. Some of us are more versatile than others, but this trait can be developed with practice by learning how to identify different social styles and relate better to persons who have a social style different from your own. Everyone is always more comfortable with a person who has the same social style as their own. Conversely, you are the least comfortable with a person who has a social style that is diagonally the opposite of yours. Development of smooth and positive interactions with others can only reinforce and magnetize your unforgettable and memorable persona.

Modifying Your Behavior to Mesh

To reinforce and magnify the memorable image you are creating, it is most important to learn how to adjust your behaviors to fit with those of the people with whom you are interacting and communicating.

Once you have identified the social style of the person with whom you are meeting, you can modify your behavior to better mesh with the social style of the other person. Often the person with whom you are talking will not know what the difference is in your approach, but he will perceive an assenting difference and frequently will show a different and positive overall reaction.

The key factor to increase your poise is to ease into change in your behaviors and actions. The idea is not to change your social style or imitate the other person's style, but rather to modify your behavior (style) in such a way as to compliment the social style of the person with whom you are speaking.

For example, if you are working with an outgoing person, a person with an expressive social style, add some excitement to your reactions and statements. You will want to give enthusiastic responses and applaud positively to comments made by your colleague. When working with an analytical person, give only the facts and data requested, and use charts and graphs to clearly show how the data is measured or evaluated. For people with an analytical social style, always provide the pros and cons for each study or data you mention, and be certain to include the sources for each of your responses.

With a driver personality, explain the project or issue quickly and concisely. When talking with a person with a driver social style, avoid giving extraneous information, especially information that is personal or unrelated to the issue being discussed. You will want to list all options that are available with the project or topic and then wait for a decision from the driver. Don't deluge the driver with facts when giving the information, but do have data and backup information available, if needed.

When working with someone with an amiable social style, building a relationship is key to success. People with an amiable social style do want to know the details of an issue, but they will focus first on developing or strengthening their relationships with others. Before discussing the issue at hand, do take some time and casually talk about issues that may be of interest to this person with an amiable social style. In this discussion, it is best to initially spend some time on personal conversation. You can comment on a painting in the office, the photo on his desk, or the colorful tie he is wearing.

The biggest problem when working with people with an amiable social style is their inability to make a decision or hold to a decision once made. You must first convince this person that the decision you are suggesting is safe, secure, and appropriate for the situation. You must strongly, but calmly reinforce to the amiable person that you are counting on him to fulfill or complete the task. And you must reassure him that he can count on you to back him up in meetings and discussions focusing on the decision he makes.

The Power of Concentration
When working in a difficult or on a challenging project, one way to maintain your poise is through focused

concentration. One idea suggested in the literature is to hold one word in your mind when you are overly stressed. If you are feeling stressed or overwhelmed with an issue or problem, stop and concentrate on one word to help you refocus. For instance, you can think of the word "hope" or "blessings." Maintaining the power of concentration helps keep the word in your mind while you maintain composure and self-control.

Nancy Jandin, a young woman with a mixed connective tissue disease, applied and was admitted to medical school. A year after starting the strenuous program, she became very ill, unable to walk more than a few feet without stopping to catch her breath. Diagnosed with pulmonary hypertension, a bleak picture was painted by her providers, but she wanted to finish school and offer medical care as she felt it should occur, so she continued. She shared her love and support with the entire class, hoping to encourage each member of the class to remember that the life of a terminally ill person needed to be lived to the fullest. Each day she attended school, oxygen in tow until she experienced several episodes where she passed out. She took a leave of absence and traveled to a lower altitude where she continued to learn and study until the last days of her life. She was honored by her class and friends as the "Wind Beneath Their Wings."

With poise, you learn how to act and react without losing composure. You need to think of yourself as a person with infinite possibilities. When you have infinite or endless possibilities, you can open doors in unbelievable ways, giving the ability to create a new and different way of reacting to challenging situations or experiences.

Ask yourself, how is my self-care? What are you doing to support and to help yourself maintain your poise and skills? If you are working in a highly pressured situation or environment, find yourself arriving from a stressful commute, or have had a negative encounter with someone, you need to take time to step back and relax before continuing participation in other events of the day. Sometimes by keeping a low profile, you can observe what is happening without becoming fully involved, yet be part of the team using a reassuring, peaceful manner. Or you may wish to go into your office for five minutes of quiet meditation—to close your eyes and concentrate on one word, allowing your mind and body to escape before going back as a helpful team player.

Allow yourself to focus on the issues that led to the stressful feeling that you are sensing and to understand how you responded to the event that created this feeling. Was the event avoidable? If not, was your participation in the event necessary and to what degree? Could you have managed the situation differently? In other words, you cannot change every event or experience in your life, but you can attempt to change your responses and behaviors when appropriate. Escaping through concentrated thought may be just the right way to help resolve or release the tension or stress produced by the situation. Let it go!

Maintaining poise while under pressure is a great skillful ability, and one that you can learn to apply more effectively. Keeping your stress level down and maintaining clear headedness will help you prevent illness or better manage a chronic disease. Learning to complement and enhance your social style will increase your poise and abilities to be an unforgettable person. Having self-control and being able to remain poised and coolheaded will make you the person everyone at the office and at home wants to have on their team, with or without a crisis. Often, I am asked how I am able to maintain a positive attitude every day on a regular basis. I don't do it any better than you. I work at it daily, and as I stated earlier, each of us is open to improvement. We are all "a work in progress."

SUMMARY THOUGHTS FROM CHAPTER EIGHT

Poise Teaches Us.....

- **With poise, you learn how to act and react without losing composure.**

- **Three steps to achieve peace of mind**

  1) Accept 100 percent responsibility for your decisions.

  2) Prioritize your activities.

  3) Concentrate your efforts on one activity at a time.

- **Determine your social style.** Do you have an expressive, a driver, an analytical, or an amiable social style? To be more effective, learn how to identify your social style and the social styles of colleagues and co-workers.

- **Modify your behavior to better mesh with the social style of the person with whom you are meeting.** Often the person you are talking with will not know what the difference is in your approach, but he or she will perceive an affirmative difference, and frequently will show a positive overall reaction.

- **One way to maintain poise is through focused concentration.** When overly stressed, focus on one word. Having the power of concentration will keep this thought in your mind while you maintain composure and self-control.

CHAPTER NINE

UNLOCKING YOUR POTENTIAL FOR CIVIC RESPONSIBILITY

There are many individuals who stand out in our minds for things that they have done to improve the communities in which we live, work, and play. There are the anonymous benefactors who through generous contributions make education available to people with lesser means. Individuals who develop programs for special needs groups many times after suffering hardships themselves, wonderful families who always find the time and space for one more child, or teachers who go the extra mile to help children achieve their greatest potential. The most memorable and unforgettable people are those who reach out to help others when often they are barely getting by themselves.

Now in our challenging political and religious climate, when individuals often seem more focused on themselves than on the collective population, these memorable people shine even brighter. Imagine what the world would be like if each one of us was willing to help two individuals achieve or be more successful through our positive encouragement, a donation of time or money, or by offering an opportunity to expand and grow through work or civic events.

Being civic-minded is to be concerned with public interests or to be active in community affairs. Civic-mindedness or civic engagement can be described as individual interests or actions that discover and work to resolve public or community issues of concern. For many, going to work each day and then attending to your family takes a majority of your time. Yet you see others in the community who go to work, spend time with their families, and still have time to contribute to community events or participate in a community outreach effort. Why are they different? How or why are some of us willing to be more involved with community efforts? Some of us are motivated by personal interests and find this time rejuvenating and rewarding. Others participate in activities in their children's school in order to meet the shortfalls left by budget issues. Do you want to help and serve as a positive role model in your neighborhood?

Civic-mindedness can lead to volunteerism, organizational or community involvement, or participation in the political process. Are you ready to participate? Most of us have 2–3 hours each month that could be set aside to bring hope, kindness, and opportunity to our neighborhoods and communities.

Please list below some of the assets and skills that you can share in your community:

_____

_____

_____

_____

_____

Involving Yourself in Public Concerns

Participation in public life or helping with common work in ways that promote the well-being of others is another way to describe civic engagement. Addressing public concerns or issues of importance that affect the well-being of our land and our lives is something that should worry or be of interest to all of us. In the 2008 presidential primary, when speaking in Portsmouth, New Hampshire, Senator Hilary Clinton challenged Americans to "take responsibility to achieve energy independence and to end global warming." Clinton stated, "This is a moment of profound change and challenge for our nation," adding that "If we do this right, it can be a win-win for our economy and our environment." Cleaning up the community around your home or workplace or working to reduce global warming will help you be involved in activities that will make a definite impact with change. Are you willing to move in that direction now?

Over the past many years, a change has been occurring in American society relative to social capital or civic-mindedness. Social capital relates to the way in which our lives are made better through social involvement, through collaboration of efforts with others in our community or organization. Mirriam-Webster's Dictionary does not include a definition for social capital. The Center for Disease Control and Prevention defines social capital as "the individual and communal time and energy that is available for such things as community improvement, social networking, civic engagement, personal recreation, and other activities that create social bonds between individuals and groups."

Wikipedia, the free encyclopedia, describes social capital as "a core concept in business, economics, organizational behaviour, political science and sociology, defined as the advantage created by a person's location in a structure of relationships." The core idea of social capital theory is that social networks have value. This concept is also described in Malcolm Gladwell's book *The Tipping Point*, where he describes how effective or destructive a single incident or individual can be— quite literally affecting most of the world population.

As Robert Putnam describes in his book *Bowling Alone*, "For the past two-thirds of the twentieth century a powerful tide bore Americans into ever deeper engagement in the life of their communities, but a few decades ago, silently, without warning, that tide reversed and we were overtaken by a treacherous rip current. Without at first noticing, we have been pulled apart from one another and from our communities over the last third of the century." He points out that many forms of social capital such as ties to family, friends, civic associations, political parties, labor unions, and religious groups have been in decline in the United States. In *Bowling Alone*, Putnam explores the causes and consequences of these changes and discusses the factors that have played significant roles in the erosion of social capital.

Civic-mindedness or involvement no longer commands the level of commitment it once held among society— among all of us. And yet, to preserve and maintain the beauty of your neighborhoods, your community, your country, and your world, and to create memorability, you need to resurrect a willingness to work for the good of the whole. You must recognize and acknowledge that your neighborhoods, your schools, your political parties, and your organizations do not function as well when you lack the commitment to give your time and attention to civic engagement.

What if each of us simply picked up a single piece of trash or a discarded pop can found lying along the street. In the book *Collapse*, Jared Diamond makes this point quite clearly showing that societies that adapt their ways of life to their geographical environment live on and last while societies that abuse environmental resources fail. It is painful to see individuals destroy the delicate world in which we live, but is also incredibly heartwarming to see others working hard to restore the natural and manmade beauty in our world. Whether someone has volunteered or is forcibly required to clean up an area, the result is the same, an improved habitat and efforts that must be applauded. There is always hope if each of us will work to make the world a better place than it was when we entered it. Add to your unforgettable image by becoming an interested and active participant in activities and events in your neighborhood and community.

Appreciation for Things That Appear to Be Readily Available

As opportunities for education, healthcare, and worship become more available, populations begin to take these opportunities for granted. There is less appreciation and therefore less respect for these services. In many instances, this declining appreciation and respect leads to a form of dependency syndrome where individuals expect rather than appreciate the services that have been developed. This expectation occurs in both developed and undeveloped communities.

Memorable or unforgettable individuals live with a thankful, grateful heart, appreciating even the most basic necessities and opportunities. For personal and professional success, you must learn to be thankful and appreciative of all that you have, to see that even if you are facing a time in your life with challenges and struggles, you still have much more for which to be thankful. To be thankful for a good heart, good mind, and good health—a place to live and food to eat, family members and friends, your animal companions, a job or volunteer activity to engage your interests—all of these people, opportunities, and situations demand your grateful appreciation and thankfulness.

Linda Popov says in *A Pace of Grace*, "One of the ways to get on with our lives is through remembering to practice thankfulness throughout the day. It compels us to notice the beauty in small things, and to slow down into awareness of the gifts each day brings."

Popov believes that when you are thankful, a magnetic attraction for abundance is created, and conversely, if you are fearful, you attract stress.

The concept of magnetic attraction is the essence of *On Being Memorable* and of my belief that what you think and feel is like a magnet that attracts particular events or people into your life.

You can create a magnetic personality by changing your attitude and behaviors and by believing that you are unlimited in all aspects of your life. Think of abundance and gratitude and use the law of attraction in everything that you do.

Based on past experiences, I believe that anyone absolutely can attract positive outcomes by making changes in his or her attitudes and behaviors. I bet that you have experienced or seen this too. Think about some remarkable change in a situation when you or someone in your group changed his or her approach and created a totally different outcome. This same type of change can occur when you apply the STAR Approach to your activities and behaviors. Creating an unforgettable, memorable image requires persistent application and reinforcement of your positive strengths. If you will begin using this approach in community efforts and activities, you will create and maintain a most memorable and unforgettable image.

Social Entrepreneurism

Another way to create an unforgettable image is to become an outgoing and dynamic social entrepreneur. Becoming an entrepreneur is one way to change your life, but this change requires hard work and ongoing persistence to achieve the goals you have established. As David Bornstein says in his book *How to Change the*

World, "What business entrepreneurs are to the economy, social entrepreneurs are to social change." His book describes memorable people who are working hard to create changes in the world where governments have failed to resolve or fix a problem.

Social entrepreneurs are people who derive innovative and creative solutions or remedies to resolve acute and chronic social problems in our society. Recently, while talking with my nephew Matt Wehling, an accomplished maker of bows for musical instruments, he described an international group working on a social entrepreneurism project. The IPCI-USA is the International Pernambuco Conservation Initiative in the United States working with a membership composed of musicians, violin and bow makers, music lovers, and conservationists. This not-for-profit organization is dedicated to the conservation and sustainable use of a Brazilian tree commonly known as Pernambuco or Pau-brazil. The Pernambuco tree grows near Rio Pardo in southern Bahia with flowers, seedpods, and roughly textured bark.

The heartwood of this tree has been used by violin makers for over 250 years and is known to bow makers and musicians alike as pernambuco wood. The tree's native habitat is located in the Brazilian Atlantic Forest and has been reduced dramatically from its original size, and the tree is becoming increasingly rare. The International Pernambuco Conservation Organization is dedicated to reversing these negative outcomes through research, replanting programs, educational outreach, and other conservation measures. Membership in the IPCI is engaged in a moratorium of any new purchases of pernambuco wood, and members provide financial support to the causes of this international world-changing movement. One goal of the IPCI is to find other sources of wood that can be used for the making of violins and bows for musical instruments.

Another wonderful example of social entrepreneurism is noted with William Shore, who is the founder and director of Share Our Strength, a national not-for-profit organization. Since 1984, this organization has raised millions of dollars to reduce poverty and eliminate hunger. In his book *The Light of Conscience: How a Simple Act Can Change Your Life*, Shore describes his concerns about our ability to cope with and manage the challenging individual and social issues in our world. His concerns focus on our ability to listen to our conscience and direct our actions accordingly. He gives examples of decisions made by many, including Rosa Parks, Mario Morino, and Matthew Lukwiya.

Social entrepreneurs find issues or problems that are not working and create a solution by changing the process or function, engineering an entirely new approach or solution. Becoming a change agent can establish a remarkably unforgettable image, but working to create change is difficult and challenging, requiring vision and persistence—sometimes only to achieve a tiny fraction or portion of a project. Are you a change agent? A quote from Napolean Hill's book *Think and Grow Rich* fits here well: "If you cannot do great things, do small things in a great way." Indeed!

Service Learning

Another focus or aspect of civic responsibility is the concept of service learning. Service learning can be defined as empowering young people to take leadership roles by providing service in their communities. It differs from traditional community service in that the planning and implementation of the service project is designed to meet specific learning objectives and involve teens throughout the project. And in service learning, evaluation and follow-up on the project occurs throughout and at the completion of the project to make certain that learning actually does occur with the teens who are involved. Have you considered helping out with a service project in your neighborhood or community?

Almost all communities have service learning projects now, and participating in such a project can be a worthwhile activity. Not only do you have the opportunity to help your community, but you also can be a positive role model for the youth involved in the project. Service learning reinforces the point that young people are valuable resources in our communities and that through their energy and skills significant changes can be made in neighborhoods to the benefit of all who live there. Two great websites offering information about service learning projects are: www.volunteermatch.org and www.nationalservice.gov. Check it out! You can become an unforgettable role model and teacher in your community!

About Being a Volunteer

Volunteerism is the willingness of people in a community to work on behalf of others in the community without expectation of pay or reimbursement through tangible gains. In all contemporary communities, the most basic of all values and concepts of community services is people helping other people (and in turn helping themselves). Are you a volunteer? All of us know memorable and unforgettable people who volunteer their time, skills and experience, or money to assist community projects. Yet how many of us sit on the sidelines and find lots of pointless excuses to avoid participating in such activities?

Do you help plant trees, read to children or the elderly, act as a docent in a museum, serve at a soup kitchen on holidays, or when traveling, collect soaps and shampoos for the homeless? Nine-eleven brought forward many volunteers who set an example of what can be accomplished through humanity, but is it really necessary to wait for a disaster to get involved? I don't think so. Do check out volunteer opportunities in your community, sign up and create a memorable opportunity in your life.

Volunteering can be accomplished as a charitable contribution, a community service, or a vocation. Possibly, volunteering can become your favorite hobby. When volunteers use their professional skills, the term "skills-based volunteerism" is used to describe this activity. Skills-based volunteerism is different from generic volunteerism where specific skills are not needed, and volunteers are simply asked to give just good old-fashioned help.

The benefits of volunteering are twofold. First, economic benefits are activities that are usually funded by the community or state government and help reduce the level of spending within the community or government. Second, social volunteering builds a more inner-connected community creating levels of collaboration and trust among community members that lead to greater stability and solidarity. When you volunteer, social capital is represented through the economic redevelopment of a community or neighborhood where friends and neighbors offer to help in times of adversity.

Sometimes a particular event or community activity may attract your attention, and you will see an opportunity where your expertise and talents can truly benefit a cause. It may be an opportunity to do something new and different or to do what you always do, but with a new and different outcome that will help meet the needs in your community.

Or it may be that the real reason you participate as a community volunteer is not simply to be memorable.

Doing good in your neighborhood or community is something that best comes from the heart and soul, rather than the need to be recognized. But once you've put your heart and soul into a project, the positive, good feelings you enjoy will help you create a more memorable impression. C'mon, c'mon—sign up soon to participate as a volunteer in your town!

List below the facilities or organizations where your assets or skills may be the most useful:

_____

_____

_____

_____

_____

Are you willing to call one or more of these organizations or facilities this week to see what you can do to help and support a good cause in your community?

Altruism

Many unforgettable people are those who make a difference in the world that creates a ripple across larger communities and the world. An altruistic person is someone who shows an unselfish regard for or devotion to the welfare of others, sometimes at their own expense—an individual who helps his neighbor shovel snow or change a tire or a choir member who helps a fellow church member or co-worker with a major life crisis. Heroes are also altruistic persons and provide great role models to help change the world by doing the right thing even though they often go unrecognized.

Often altruistic individuals set out to change popular thinking by introducing a method that is not accepted as a way to accomplish things. In doing so, they can and do change history, but their path is often difficult and fraught with criticism and condemnation. One good example, a small number of medical educators set out to change the way physicians are educated in order to make a difference in the way that these doctors will practice medicine. Their approach was one of nurturing support to help the doctor become a wonderful practitioner and an asset to society and medicine. Initially, their approach met with significant criticism, but the educators persevered creating an approach to medical education in the United States that thirty years later has become a natural approach to medical education and problem-based learning. The altruistic nature of these educators made the difference in numerous lives—in the lives of the individuals trained in their programs, and in the lives of countless patients who were touched by this unique approach to medical education and the medical providers who were developed through it.

Oprah Winfrey is such a wonderful example of someone who works to be the best that she can be, but also accepts that she works with the same weaknesses that all of us cope with every day. The tabloids are quick to point out her weaknesses and present her as a failure. Yet she gives so much to so many less fortunate people. Oprah responds with honesty and frankness, sharing her successes and her struggles with the world without shame. Wow! What a memorable and unforgettable person!

Differing Viewpoints
Open-mindedness is clearly a primary ingredient necessary when helping others and promoting change

in the community. Within the realm of civic duty, one aspect of social responsibility is the respect of all persons involved in a community or civic project. Often you may find yourself working on a project with individuals who "aren't like you" or who "don't think the way you do." You may ignore this person or react coolly to attempts at conversation in an attempt to distance yourself so that others will not think you are associated with this person. But here is where morality and manners must come in full force. Open-mindedness applies not only to the project of planting and tending a community garden for disadvantaged persons who live across town, but also to treating these persons with respectful behaviors and good manners.

Open-mindedness is defined as being receptive to new and different ideas or the opinions of others; of having an open-minded impartiality. Being open-minded does not mean being easily influenced by the ideas and opinions of others, but it does mean being inclined to respect the views and beliefs that are different from our own and to treat with respect and good manners the person offering this differing point of view. How do you rate your open-mindedness?

Each of us has standards and moral values that we believe in and live by. Consequently, you tend to feel very strongly about certain viewpoints and activities in which you believe. Thus, when you are challenged by the viewpoints of others, you often may react negatively. One of my favorite teachings by Stephen Covey is his thought, "Seek first to understand then to be understood." A great concept, but it is a hard one to apply when you have strong opinions or feelings about particular subjects.

At times, you may encounter situations like this when talking with family members whose belief systems are usually patterned just like your own. You think that you already know what will be said and how it is meant, and you may have planned a response before the other individual has even finished speaking. You respond then to what is assumed to be true and rarely think about alternative scenarios. As you may recognize, this behavior can lead to unnecessary ill feelings toward others and yourself. Learning to listen carefully and thoughtfully respond can help you create that unforgettable image you seek and prevent compounding misunderstandings.

Some topics, like religion, war, peace, corporal punishment, and abortion, are powerful and emotional issues that may cause you to react quickly without thinking through your response. Seeking to understand others offers the opportunity to move toward reconciliation of different opinions. Generally, if you consider all of the factors involved, you have far more in common than in opposition. The ability to teach yourself and help others grow through open-mindedness, experiences, and understanding can be most rewarding and beneficial—clearly a memorable option.

Learning things that you thought you knew—acknowledging that there is much in the world that you do not know or understand and the willingness to admit this truth will allow you to truly understand others and their differing points of view. Many times you will find that you share more in common regarding a controversial topic than you thought possible with another individual. A close associate once said, "The narrower the difference, the closer the span to resolution."

Recognize and reiterate those things that are common before seeking to expound on the differences. You can be an unforgettable resolver of issues. Take a chance and open your mind to new ideas and options. Who knows? It may be a most memorable experience!

Become Part of the Change

To be a remarkable and memorable person, you must be willing to give of yourself—to get up off of the couch and become involved in a community activity that benefits the good of us all. Think about the options of community projects that are available in your community and find one in which you are willing to participate. Sign up and volunteer to help! Most amazingly, once you have become involved, you will feel enormously wonderful about what you have done and about who you are.

There are many opportunities to develop or participate in activities that will help change the world. You are challenged to choose at least one activity in the coming year that will help improve life in your community. Food and shelter are necessary for life, yet many people in the world that have neither. Mothers and children are especially hard hit by these realities. Many religious sects have been persecuted over the centuries, yet little seems to have been learned by either the persecutors or the persecuted. In fact, the same negative scenarios have repeated themselves throughout history, often linked to a notion of moving toward overall improvement. Sadly, the results are the opposite, and the cycle begins again. You are a part of the future. Will you help make life better through your own commitment to civic-mindedness and responsibility?

Become the Difference—Accomplish the Change You Seek

One commonly seen quote states something to the effect that if you seek change, you should begin with (changing) yourself.   Ahhhhh, so very, very true. Yet changing ourselves is often the hardest challenge and most compelling change that you may face. That is why the STAR Approach of reinforcing your attributes and positive capabilities will become an invaluable asset as you work to create the image you desire and the image you hope to leave in the minds of those you meet and associate with.

As stated in Chapter Two, most of us did not consciously identify the image we now have. For many of us, it (the image) just sort of happened. But if you review the Summary Points made at the end of each chapter, you will see the keys, the very foundation you need for creating the changes you wish to see happen.

As stated several times throughout this book, creating a new image is not easy and requires great persistence and assiduous diligence. But after lots of hard work and a consistent change in attitude and behavior, the outcome—the desired image you seek—is most pleasing. To be that memorable, positively unforgettable person..... ooooohhhhh, so most deliciously wonderful!!!

SUMMARY THOUGHTS FROM CHAPTER NINE

You Can...........
- **Make a commitment of your time and attention** to give to your community.

- **Be willing to give your time** and take the trouble to pick up trash and plastic bags or pop cans from your neighborhood and community.

- **Become an interested and active participant** in activities and events in your neighborhood and community.

- **Be thankful every day** for the small and most wonderful things that occur in your life.

- **Become a social entrepreneur** and help create social change and a better world.

- **Participate in a service learning project** and help empower young people in your area.

- **Volunteer! Volunteer!! Volunteer!!!**

- **Learn how to have unselfish regard or devotion** to a cause that will benefit the welfare of others.

- **Learn the ability to grow** through open-mindedness, experience, and understanding.

- **Create and accomplish the changes you seek!**

CHAPTER TEN

ONE HUNDRED PLUS WAYS TO BE MEMORABLE AND UNFORGETTABLE

STAR Power—Self-Recognition

o   Smile – a lot!!!

o   Develop attuned, attentive advisers and mentors who will give you honest, critical feedback about your performance and your image.

o   Be well-read and well-informed about your profession and about issues crucial to your work, your community, or national and world event.

o   Be Happy! It is so much more fun than being sad, angry, or miserable, and it will create a positive and memorable image.

o   Be a proactive achiever—a doer—someone who moves and gets things done.

o   Have a positive attitude. A positive attitude is an essential foundation for making a most memorable impression.

o   Use humor effectively and in a positive way. It will add to your memorable image.

o   Create possibilities or options for positive outcomes.

o   Be humble; humility is good and only a negative element in your mind.

o Go the extra mile, over and over and over again.

o Find something good about each person or event that happens to you each day, and share that positive thought with others.

o Avoid thinking that in order for you to look good, you must discount or criticize another.

o Reinforce your unforgetableness by treating everyone with respect and good manners.

o Think about what you say and how you say it—words are always most memorable.

o Learn to roll with the punches and work under pressure without complaints.

o Listen attentively. Make the person you are listening to feel like he or she is the only person around.

o Give credit to others; search for something positive to praise.

o Be poised, be confident, and keep your head up when the stuff hits the fan.

o Initiate your position with a statement that supports agreement and allows or encourages others to agree with you.

o Think about what you write and how you write it—poor grammar, spelling, or typographical errors do not create the memorable image you seek.

o Practice being a star when talking on the phone with salespeople, wrong number callers, or when taking a message for others.

o   Be prepared for meetings and appointments. People will think that you are ineffective when you are disorganized or muddled with your thoughts.

o   Add a new word to your vocabulary each week; write the word on paper and post it on your fridge or desk to remind you to use it.

o   Learn to use power thoughtfully, judiciously, and effectively.

o   Be flexible and learn to compromise; be able to change and have resiliency.

o   Persist and complete difficult jobs or projects; your co-workers and supervisors will notice and remember you positively.

o   Avoid arguments; learn to discuss differences and deliberate issues; keep the discussion impersonal and attack the issue, not the person.

o   Be consistent and pay attention to details.

o   Admit errors quickly when you are wrong; you will not be blamed for being wrong as much as you will be admired for admitting your mistake.

o   Give up tired, old routines and adapt quickly to change—be an innovator, not a laggard.

o   Begin discussions in a friendly tone; smile warmly and give needed information to listeners.

o   Eliminate envy and the discussions that accompany this feeling; be positive about the good fortunes of others.

- o Develop a signature look or style—everyday wear a turtleneck, bow tie, or distinctive pin, or always wear a hat; make it your own.

- o Use your imagination. Don't be traditional in your thinking or your approach.

- o Remember names and use a person's name whenever possible.

- o Use your local library and read one book each month.

- o Dramatize your ideas with short stories or examples that reinforce your point.

- o Be on time for appointments—memorable people show their commitment by being there and you don't have to begin the conversation with the words, "I'm sorry for being late."

- o Ask stimulating questions, causing yourself and others to think while creating a more memorable impression of yourself.

- o Listen to your conscience and do the right things; accept the responsibility of being conscientious, virtuous, and principled in the way you conduct your life.

- o Treat yourself to hope, inspiration, and encouragement from like-minded friends.

- o Seize the possibilities in your life. Go for it!!!

STAR Power—Reach Out to Others

- o Share power and information with others, giving them the opportunity to reach conclusions, solve problems, and justify decisions.

- o Look into the eyes of others when you speak to them.

- o When you're out of town, mail a card to your office staff thanking them for keeping the office running smoothly.

- o Send a congratulatory note to friends and acquaintances mentioned for a promotion, new job, new baby, or who have received an award.

- o Be aware of the attitudes and beliefs of your audience, and adjust your comments to the person or group with whom you are speaking.

- o Following a job interview, send a note thanking the interviewer for the opportunity of meeting and for the time given during the interview.

- o Treat secretaries, support staff, and mailroom staff warmly and with respect; know their names and use them when you say hello or ask questions.

- o Write a thoughtful article for your company newsletter or for a professional or trade journal.

- o Tell someone, by telephone or in person, how delighted you are to hear their voice or see them.

o If you have a complaint to present at a meeting or to your boss, be certain to have a solution to offer that will help resolve the issue.

o At the end of each day, thank your staff for being present and for doing a great job.

o When dining out, call the waitress or waiter by name, be attentive when they serve, and thank them personally before you leave.

o Send a thank you note to anyone who helps you, personally or professionally.

o Ask others about their children, invalid mother, or favorite pet, and listen to their response.

o After a business or social function, give all of the leftover food to the local mission.

o During the holiday season, give a thank you note and small box of chocolates or mints to the garbage takers, clothing cleaners, mail person, or others who help throughout the year.

o Call your mother or another very important person and say, "I love you."

o Make others feel unique—create or reinforce special feelings in another person.

o When a bus boy or girl clears the restaurant table, quietly give him or her a small gratuity as a thank you for services; likewise when staying overnight in a hotel, leave a gratuity for the housekeeping person.

o Read the name tags on grocery or department store staff to say hello or address the check-out staff person by name.

STAR Power—Share Yourself

o Give to others—your time, ideas, support, or assistance. Help an organization or agency in your community.

o Join a friend for dinner, or ask someone new to join you because it is a new way to give.

o When asked for your opinion, thoughtfully state your position. Whether for or against, you will be respected for being willing to share your thoughts.

o Give your time to a community organization or group that needs volunteer help.

o Send a note to your widowed aunt or uncle, grandparents, or dear old friends remembering good times with them.

o Give compliments to the people around you. You may notice and admire others all day long, but frequently fail to share this important information with the person admired.

o Accept gifts or compliments gracefully and tell the giver how pleased you are with the gift or comment.

o Foster a spirit of generosity. A giving of one's self is one of the best gifts, and as you give of yourself, you receive peace and blessings from a Higher Power.

STAR Power—Have Fun

- o Learn a language distinct from the one you use and speak it, every day.

- o Invent a new widgit and sell it to millions, and then use some of your wealth to help establish state of the art, animal-friendly shelters for dogs and cats.

- o Speak in Pig Latin to people other than your children.

- o Fill out and complete research survey forms that come in your mail seeking information about environmental, political, or other issues.

- o Drive an old, but elegantly restored classic car, or drive a jalopy and love it.

- o Sort through old clothes, dishes, and bedding finding useful pieces for community groups helping disadvantaged people.

- o Dress in costume on Halloween to answer the door for trick-or-treaters.

- o Ask each member of a committee on which you serve to bring one can of food to each meeting and take the cans to a local mission each month.

- o For one year, dye your hair a different color every month.

- o Take the time to write a note telling a company about an outstanding employee or about the provision of a customer-friendly service.

- o Each month, attend a different church in your community to learn lessons from others.

o Attend a book club. If none exists, start one and ask favorite and interesting people to join you.

o Get a college degree, an MBA or a PhD for your seventy-fifth birthday.

o Learn a few words in French or Italian and use them when you go to the French bakery or Italian market.

o Support the local sports teams in your town or community.

STAR Power—Beautify Your World

- Hang original artwork or quality reproductions in your office and waiting room.

- Use the local recyclers for paper, plastic, and cans.

- Create a perennial flower garden in the front of your home or office to distinguish the building from others on the block.

- When it is cold and snowy, buy a sweater for your dog and be sure she/he wears it on trips outside.

- Get Mondays off to a great start by bringing cut flowers to your office or send a small bouquet to your secretary or a favorite person in your life.

- Beautifully decorate the outside of your home for the holidays.

- Plant a tree—trees add beauty to the outdoors and help our world stay clean.

- Be creative with the image in your office and with your notes and memos. Find a look that you love and use it to create a memorable image.

- Help a friend by cleaning her garden and planting rose bushes in a newly created flower bed.

- Create sunflower wreaths to give family and friends for the birds in their yards.

- Shovel the snow from walks and driveways for older neighbors or friends.

- Use a break-free collar with a bell and nametag for your most charming cat friends.

- Organize a workday with your neighbors to pick up trash and keep your street and parks clean.

STAR Power—In Action

- o Thank God or a Higher Power for your good health, good heart, and good mind.

- o Be reliable and follow through on commitments and promises made. Be known as someone who always comes through—in or out of a crunch.

- o Smile—a lot! At everyone, from friends to strangers, to everyone you see.

- o Be wonderfully enthusiastic. Enthusiasm moves others, powerfully!

- o Pay close attention to detail and consistency. Often you will remember the big things and do them well. Yet it is the small stuff, the subtleties that will make you memorable, both positively and negatively.

- o In order to be memorable, you do not have to do Herculean things; you just need to be a little bit better than average, and you will stand out most positively.

Adopt the STAR Approach—Go Ahead and Shine!!!

RESOURCES

Aristotle, and J. Barnes. *The Complete Works of Aristotle: Revised Oxford Translation: Volume One*. Princeton, NJ: Princeton University Press, 1984.

Bennett, William. *The Book of Virtues*. New York: Simon & Schuster, 1993.

Birysenko, Joan, and Gordon Dveirin. *Saying Yes to Change: Essential Wisdom for Your Journey*. Carlsbad, CA: Hay House, 2005.

Bornstein, David. *How to Change the World*. New York: Oxford University Press, 2004.

Covey, Stephen. *First Things First*. New York: Simon & Schuster, 2003.

Covey, Stephen. *The 7 Habits of Highly Effective People*. New York: Simon & Schuster, 1989.

Diamond, Jared. *Collapse*. New York: Penguin Books, 2005.

Durant, Will, and Ariel Durant. *The Lessons of History*. New York: Simon & Schuster, 1968.

Dyer, Wayne. *The Power of Intention*. Carlsbad, CA: Hay House, 2004

Eisen, Armand. *Words of Wisdom*. New York: Ariel Books, 1992.

Franklin, Benjamin. *The Art of Virtue*. Eden Prairie, MN: Acorn Publishing, 1986.

Gladwell, Malcolm. *The Tipping Point*. New York: Back Bay Books, 2002.

Hamilton, Edith, and Huntington Cairns, eds. *The Collected Dialogues of Plato*. Princeton, NJ: Princeton University Press, 1961.

Heider, John. *The Tao of Leadership*. New York: Bantam Books, 1985.

Hesse, Hermann. *Siddartha*. New York: New Directions, 1951.

Hill, Napoleon. *Think and Grow Rich*. Chatsworth, CA: Wilshire Book Company, 1966.

Hill, Napoleon. *The Master Key to Riches*. New York: Fawcett Crest Books, 1945.

Jones, Thomas. *Words of Wisdom*. Chicago: J.G. Ferguson, 1966.

Lauer, Charles S. *Soar with the Eagles*. Walla Walla, WA: Coffee Communications, Inc., 1991.

Maguire, Daniel. *The Moral Choice*. Minneapolis, MN: Winston Press, 1975.

Maxwell, John. *Thinking for a Change*. New York: Warner Business Books, 2003.

Merriam-Webster's Collegiate Dictionary. Eleventh Edition. Springfield, Massachusetts, 2006

Merrill, David, and Roger Reid. *Personal Styles and Effective Performance*. Boca Raton, FL: CRC Books, 1981.

Merton, Thomas. *Thoughts in Solitude*. Boston: Shambhala, 1993.

Musashi, Miyamoto. *A Book of Five Rings*. Woodstock, NY: Overlook Press, 1974.

Native American Wisdom. Philadelphia: Running Press, 1993.

Orman, Suze. *The 9 Steps to Financial Freedom.* Philadelphia: Running Press, 2001.

Patov, Linda. *A Pace of Grace.* New York: Plume Books, 2004.

Peale, Norman Vincent. *The Power of Positive Thinking.* New York: Ballantine Books, 1996.

Putnam, Robert. *Bowling Alone.* New York: Simon & Schuster, 2000.

Rischer, Louis, ed. *The Essential Gandhi.* New York: Vintage, 1962.

Ryan, M. J. *A Grateful Heart.* New York: Fine Communications, 1997.

Shore, William H. *The Light of Conscience: How a Simple Act Can Change Your Life.* New York: Random House,2004.

Shore, William H. *The Cathedral Within: Transforming Your Life by Giving Something Back.* New York: Random House, 2001.

Smith, Joseph. *The Book of Mormon.* Salt Lake City, UT: The Church of Jesus Christ of Latter Day Saints. 1986.

Smith, Steve, ed. *Ways of Wisdom.* Lanham, MD: University Press, 1983.

Tao: To Know and Not be Knowing. Rock Springs, WY: Labyrinth Publishing, 1993.

The Holy Bible

The Wisdom of Confucius. New York: Peter Pauper Press, 1963.

Waley, Arthur, trans. *The Analect of Confucius.* New York: Vintage, 1938.

Zen: The Reason of Unreason. Rock Springs, WY: Labyrinth Publishing, 1993.

ABOUT THE AUTHOR

Ruthie H. Dearing, MHSA, JD

Ruthie H. Dearing has an advanced educational background in management, healthcare systems and the law. For twenty years, she was founder and president of Dearing & Associates, Inc. a healthcare consulting firm specializing in market research, program design and implementation, and promotion and advertising of women and children's healthcare programs.

She has published numerous articles on marketing strategies and healthcare programming for women. In 1987, Ruthie was the primary author of Marketing Women's Healthcare, the first book published in the U.S. that focused on marketing healthcare services to women.

Ruthie is a frequent motivational speaker with a wide range of topics emphasizing strategies for achieving personal and professional success. Other presentations assist business owners with improved productivity and enhanced interest among employees, small groups or large. In her "Being Memorable" presentation, Ruthie notes that personal presence and credibility do not just automatically happen. This presentation concentrates on the nine keys that will help you accomplish the full benefit of unforgettable memorability, whether on the job or in your personal life.

Although Ruthie now enjoys living in Albuquerque, New Mexico, she misses Washington State where she lived in Spokane for almost 25 years. For information about presentations, please contact her at:
dearing.associates@gmail.com

4600802

Made in the USA
Charleston, SC
17 February 2010